150 Fun-to-Stitch Projects

Edited by Laura Scott

HOUSE of
WHITE
BIRCHES
PUBLISHERS
SINCE 1947

Editor: Laura Scott
Associate Editor: June Sprunger
Copy Editor: Cathy Reef

Photography: Tammy Christian, Nora Elsesser, Teri Staub
Photography Assistants: Linda Quinlan, Arlou Witwer

Production Manager: Vicki Macy
Creative Coordinator: Shaun Venish
Book Design/Production: Dan Kraner
Traffic Coordinator: Sandra Beres
Production Assistants: Shirley Blalock, Dana Brotherton,
Carol Dailey, Cheryl Lynch, Jessica Rothe, Miriam Zacharias

Publishers: Carl H. Muselman, Arthur K. Muselman
Chief Executive Officer: John Robinson
Marketing Director: Scott Moss
Editorial Director: Vivian Rothe
Production Director: Scott Smith

Printed in the United States of America
First Printing: 1998
Library of Congress Number: 97-76986
ISBN: 1-882138-33-3

Every effort has been made to ensure the accuracy and completeness of the
instructions in this book. However, we cannot be responsible for human
error or for the results when using materials other than those specified in
the instructions, or for variations in individual work.

Introduction

What a delight it has been to put this book together for you! Between juggling our spouses, children, careers, friends, household duties and the endless list of "to-dos," there is often precious little time to devote to our favorite hobby—plastic canvas. This book brings you more than 150 (we managed to squeeze in a few extras for you!) all-new plastic canvas projects that are truly fun to stitch.

It's important to experience the feeling of completion and accomplishment that comes from finishing an entire project. With this book, you'll find dozens upon dozens of projects that will give you this kind of satisfaction, many after just a couple hours of stitching.

Plus, this delightful collection covers the gamut of projects from fast and fun bazaar items and tissue box covers, to home decorating accents and gifts for family and friends from age 1 to 101, to projects for your kids and decorations to make your Christmas season festive and cheerful year after year. It is my hope that this book is where you first turn to whenever you have a craft sale, gift-giving occasion or simply are looking for a new project to begin.

You'll find most of the projects in this collection use the ever-popular 7-count plastic canvas and worsted-weight or plastic canvas yarn. For those who enjoy more detailed work, we've included a smattering of 10- and 14-count plastic canvas projects.

All of us who worked together to bring you this book wish you many relaxing and rewarding hours of pleasant plastic canvas stitching.

Warmest regards,

Laura Scott

Laura Scott, Editor
150 Fun-to-Stitch Projects

Contents

Chapter 3: *Terrific Tissue Toppers*

Chapter 1: *Bazaar Bestsellers*

Chapter 4: *Gifts Galore*

Chapter 2: *Easy Home Accents*

Chapter 5: Kid-Pleasing Projects

Chapter 6: The Spirit of Christmas

General Information

Bazaar Best Sellers

Get those stitching fingers ready to create dozens of fun projects sure to bring in the profits at your next craft show or church bazaar! This colorful chapter includes many bazaar favorites such as magnets, plant pokes, mini-baskets, ornaments, bookmarks and much more!

Fun With Magnets

Quick and easy to stitch, magnets are the perfect project for bazaar selling success. Our pretty Button Fan and Beaded Heart magnets will please those with an elegant, feminine decor. Kids will love seeing their school picture in the clever ABC Photo Frame magnet, and Honey Do is perfect for leaving gentle reminders to your spouse.

Honey Do

Skill Level: Beginner

Materials
- ¼ sheet 7-count plastic canvas
- Uniek Needloft plastic canvas yarn as listed in color key
- DMC #3 pearl cotton as listed in color key
- #16 tapestry needle
- #18 tapestry needle
- 2" magnetic strip
- Orange plastic paper clip
- Hot-glue gun

Instructions

1. Cut out plastic canvas according to the graph (page 8).

2. Stitch piece following graph. Work black yarn Straight Stitch and white pearl cotton Backstitches over completed background stitching. Overcast ears with cinnamon and remaining edges with adjacent colors following graph.

3. Using photo as a guide, center and glue paper clip to lower backside, allowing part of the clip to hang down below bottom of stitched piece. Glue magnetic strip to backside of stitched piece above paper clip.

—Design by Angie Arickx

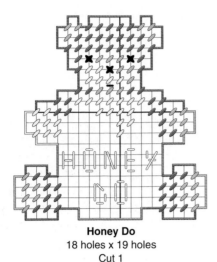

Honey Do
18 holes x 19 holes
Cut 1

```
COLOR KEY
HONEY DO
Plastic Canvas Yarn                Yards
■ Black #00                            1
■ Cinnamon #14                         3
■ Camel #43                            2
□ Yellow #57                           1
  Uncoded area is sundown
  #10 Continental Stitches             3
╱ Sundown #10 Overcasting
╱ Black #00 Straight Stitch
#3 Pearl Cotton
╱ White Backstitch                     1
Color numbers given are for Uniek Needloft
plastic canvas yarn.
```

Button Fan

Skill Level: Beginner

Materials

- Small piece 7-count white plastic canvas
- Worsted weight yarn as listed in color key
- #16 tapestry needle
- 7 (¼") ivory buttons
- ½" ivory button
- Sewing needle and ivory sewing thread
- Pink felt
- 1" magnetic strip
- Craft glue

Instructions

1. Cut plastic canvas according to graph. Cut felt to fit fan shape.

2. Continental Stitch piece following graph. Work dark pink Straight Stitches when background stitching is completed. Overcast with dark pink.

3. Using photo as a guide, with sewing needle and

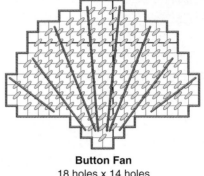

Button Fan
18 holes x 14 holes
Cut 1

```
COLOR KEY
BUTTON FAN
Worsted Weight Yarn            Yards
□ Light pink                      2
■ Dark pink Straight Stitch
  and Overcasting                 3
```

ivory thread, attach ¼" buttons to top edge of fan between Straight Stitches. Sew ½" button to base of fan.

4. Glue felt to back of stitched piece. Center and glue magnetic strip to felt.

—Design by Kathleen Marie O'Donnell

Beaded Heart

Skill Level: Intermediate

Materials

- Small piece 10-count plastic canvas
- DMC 6-strand embroidery floss as listed in color key
- #22 tapestry needle
- #26 tapestry needle
- 80 yellow glass beads
- Gold felt
- 1½" magnetic strip
- White glue

Instructions

1. Cut plastic canvas according to graph. Cut felt to fit heart shape.

2. Continental Stitch piece with 12 strands floss following graph. Overcast with 6 strands ultra light tan.

3. With 3 strands ultra light tan and #26 tapestry needle, sew beads around outside edge of heart. Come up through one hole, thread on bead and go down through next hole so that bead sits on top of canvas bars. When last bead has been attached, fasten thread securely.

4. For beaded loops at bottom, bring thread up through bottom left hole, thread on five beads and bring needle down through center hole. Bring needle up through bottom right hole, thread on five beads and bring needle down through center hole. Fasten thread securely.

5. Glue felt to back of stitched piece. Center and glue magnetic strip to felt. Allow to dry.

—Design by Kathleen Marie O'Donnell

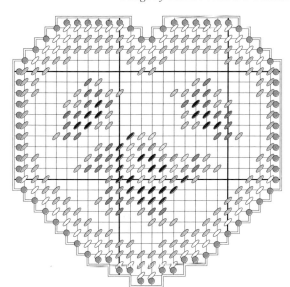

Beaded Heart
25 holes x 25 holes
Cut 1

COLOR KEY	
BEADED HEART	
6-Strand Embroidery Floss	**Yards**
■ Medium lavender #208	1
▨ Light lavender #210	1
▨ Tan brown #436	3
■ Very dark Christmas red #498	1
■ Very dark violet #550	1
■ Dark carnation #600	1
▨ Light cranberry #603	1
▨ Very light cranberry #605	1
☐ Ultra light tan #738	5
■ Dark willow green #3345	2
▨ Dark apple green #3347	1
Uncoded areas are ecru	4
Continental Stitches	
● Attach yellow bead	
Color numbers given are for DMC 6-strand embroidery floss.	

ABC Photo Frame

Skill Level: Beginner

Materials

- ½ sheet 7-count plastic canvas
- Small amount 10-count plastic canvas
- Worsted weight yarn as listed in color key
- 2 (2¼") magnetic strips
- Hot-glue gun

Instructions

1. Cut frame front and back from 7-count plastic canvas; cut apple and letters from 10-count plastic canvas according to graphs (below and page 11). Frame back and letters will remain unstitched.

2. Stitch frame front with 4 plies yarn following graph. Overcast inside edges with black. Whipstitch front to back with tan around outside edges.

3. Stitch and Overcast apple and Overcast letters with 2 plies yarn following graphs.

4. Using photo as a guide, glue letters above top left inside corner of photo opening. Glue apple below bottom right inside corner of photo opening. Glue magnetic strips to back of frame, making sure glue does not stick to frame front.

—Design by Kimberly A. Suber

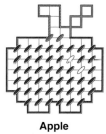

Apple
9 holes x 10 holes
Cut 1 from 10-count

COLOR KEY	
ABC PHOTO FRAME	
Worsted Weight Yarn	**Yards**
■ Black	4
▨ Tan	4
☐ White	2
■ Red	1
■ Dark brown	1
╱ Dark green Overcasting	1

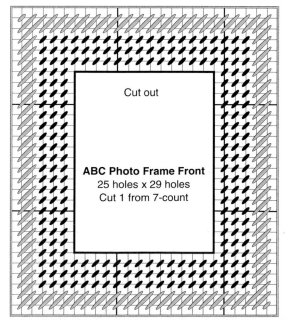

Cut out

ABC Photo Frame Front
25 holes x 29 holes
Cut 1 from 7-count

Graphs continued on page 11

Spoon Toppers

Slide these strawberry, honey and apple culinary accents over wooden spoons and arrange in a jar for a pretty kitchen decoration!

Skill Level: Beginner

Materials

- ½ sheet 7-count plastic canvas
- Spinrite Bernat Berella "4" worsted weight yarn as listed in color key
- #16 tapestry needle
- Ceramic buttons by Mill Hill Products from Gay Bowles Sales, Inc.:

  Strawberry #86079

  Beehive #86129

  Apple #86103
- Sewing needle and sewing thread to match buttons
- 18" each ⅛"-wide red, yellow and pale green ribbon
- 3 wooden spoons

Instructions

1. Cut plastic canvas according to graphs. Topper backs will remain unstitched.

2. Stitch fronts following graphs. Work embroidery using 2 plies yarn when background stitching is completed.

3. With sewing needle and matching thread, sew strawberry button to strawberry jam front where indicated on graph. Repeat for remaining two buttons, sewing beehive button to honey jar front and apple button to apple jelly front.

4. Overcast bottom edge of strawberry jam front between red dots with geranium. Whipstitch remaining edges of front to back along sides with geranium and around lid with dark lagoon. Tie red ribbon in a bow around notched edge of lid, trimming ends as desired.

5. Overcast bottom edge of honey jar front between red dots with oak. Whipstitch remaining edges of front to back along sides with oak and around lid with walnut. Tie yellow ribbon in a bow around notched edge of lid, trimming ends as desired.

6. Overcast bottom edge of apple jelly front between red dots with honey. Whipstitch remaining edges of front to back along sides with honey and around lid with scarlet. Tie pale green ribbon in a bow around notched edge of lid, trimming ends as desired.

7. Insert spoons into toppers.

—Designs by Joan Green

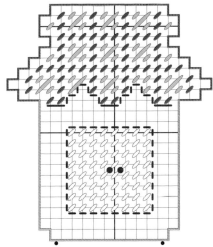

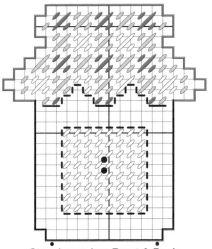

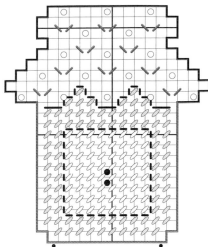

Honey Jar Front & Back
19 holes x 22 holes
Cut 2, stitch 1

Strawberry Jam Front & Back
19 holes x 22 holes
Cut 2, stitch 1

Apple Jelly Front & Back
19 holes x 22 holes
Cut 2, stitch 1

COLOR KEY
HONEY JAR

Worsted Weight Yarn	Yards
▨ Light tapestry gold #8886	1
▨ Walnut #8916	3
☐ Natural #8940	2
Uncoded areas are honey #8795 Continental Stitches	2
╱ Oak #8796 Overcasting and Whipstitching	1
╱ Black #8994 2-ply Backstitch	½
● Attach button	

Color numbers given are for Spinrite Bernat Berella "4" worsted weight yarn.

COLOR KEY
STRAWBERRY JAM

Worsted Weight Yarn	Yards
▨ Medium lagoon #8821	1
▨ Dark lagoon #8822	2
☐ Natural #8940	2
Uncoded areas are scarlet #8933 Continental Stitches	2
╱ Geranium #8929 Overcasting and Whipstitching	1
╱ Black #8994 2-ply Backstitch	½
● Attach button	

Color numbers given are for Spinrite Bernat Berella "4" worsted weight yarn.

COLOR KEY
APPLE JELLY

Worsted Weight Yarn	Yards
☐ Pale tapestry gold #8887	1½
☐ Natural #8940	2
Uncoded areas are scarlet #8933 Continental Stitches	3
╱ Honey #8795 Overcasting and Whipstitching	1
╱ Scarlet #8933 Whipstitching	
╱ Dark lagoon #8822 2-ply Backstitch	½
╱ Black #8994 2-ply Backstitch	
○ Natural #8940 2-ply French Knot	
● Attach button	

Color numbers given are for Spinrite Bernat Berella "4" worsted weight yarn.

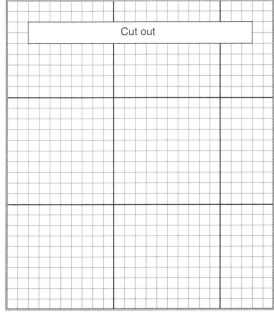

ABC Photo Frame Back
25 holes x 29 holes
Cut 1 from 7-count
Do not stitch

ABC Photo Frame

Continued from page 9

COLOR KEY
ABC PHOTO FRAME

Worsted Weight Yarn	Yards
■ Black	4
▨ Tan	4
☐ White	2
■ Red	1
▨ Dark brown	1
╱ Dark green Overcasting	1

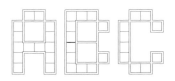

Letters
4 holes x 6 holes
Cut 1 each from 10-count
Do not stitch

Noah & Company

The biblical story of Noah is an all-time favorite among parents and children alike. Keep it and all of God's promises fresh in your family's minds with a colorful magnet and ornament.

Noah & Company Magnet

Skill Level: Beginner

Materials

- ¼ sheet 7-count plastic canvas
- Uniek Needloft plastic canvas yarn as listed in color key
- #16 tapestry needle
- 2" magnetic strip
- Hot-glue gun

Instructions

1. Cut plastic canvas according to graph.

2. Continental Stitch piece following graph. Work embroidery over completed background stitching. Overcast with royal and maple following graph.

3. Center and glue magnetic strip to backside of stitched piece.

—*Design by Angie Arickx*

God's Promise Ornament

Skill Level: Beginner

Materials

- Darice 14-count plastic canvas Crafty Circle
- DMC 6-strand embroidery floss as listed in color key

- 6" gold cord
- 2½" gold circular frame
- ½" white plastic dove #8490 from Fibre-Craft
- Index card
- Tacky craft glue

Instructions

1. Continental Stitch plastic canvas with 6 strands floss following graph.

2. Backstitch lines in boat with 2 strands tan brown. Backstitch under roof line with 2 strands coffee brown. Backstitch words with 4 strands white. Work French Knot with 2 strands white. Twist equal 6-strand lengths of blue and very light blue together and Overcast edges following graph.

3. Cut index card to fit back of frame. Glue dove to top of frame. Allow to dry. Insert stitched piece into frame.

4. Knot ends of gold cord together, forming a loop. Glue knotted ends to top backside of stitched piece. Glue index card to backside of frame.

—*Design by Janna Britton*

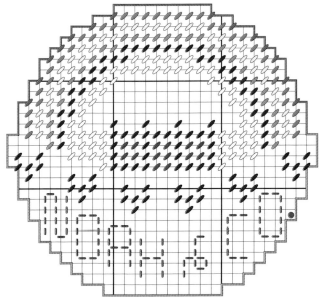

Noah & Company Magnet
29 holes x 27 holes
Cut 1

COLOR KEY	
NOAH & COMPANY MAGNET	
Plastic Canvas Yarn	**Yards**
■ Christmas red #02	3
▨ Brown #15	2
▨ Royal #32	1
☐ White #41	2
▨ Mermaid #53	1
☐ Yellow #57	1
▨ Bright orange #58	1
Uncoded areas are maple	
#13 Continental Stitches	7
⁄ Maple #13 Overcasting	
⁄ Brown #15 Backstitch	
● Brown #15 French Knot	
Color numbers given are for Uniek Needloft plastic canvas yarn.	

COLOR KEY	
GOD'S PROMISE ORNAMENT	
Plastic Canvas Yarn	**Yards**
▨ Medium lavender #208	3
▨ Coffee brown #433	4
▨ Tan brown #436	3
▨ Dark burnt orange #608	2
▨ Kelly green #701	3
☐ Dark yellow #744	2
■ Nasturtium #817	2
▨ Dark blue #825	3
▨ Very light blue #827	8¾
Uncoded area is blue #799	
Continental Stitches	8¾
⁄ Blue #799 and very light blue #827 Overcasting	
⁄ White 4-strand Backstitch	2
○ White 2-strand French Knot	
⁄ Coffee brown #433 2-strand Backstitch	
⁄ Tan brown #436 2-strand Backstitch	
Color numbers given are for DMC 6-strand embroidery floss.	

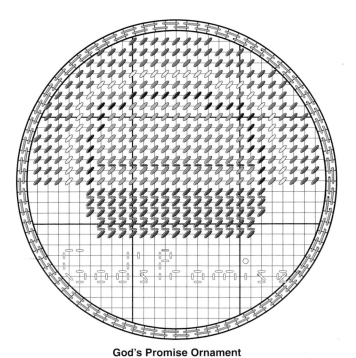

God's Promise Ornament
Stitch 1

Birdhouse Ornament

Whether you hang this delightful birdhouse in a sunny window or on your Christmas tree, it is sure to add a touch of sweet country charm to your home!

Skill Level: Beginner

Materials

- ½ sheet 7-count plastic canvas
- Darice Nylon Plus plastic canvas yarn as listed in color key
- DMC 6-strand embroidery floss as listed in color key
- #16 tapestry needle
- ¾" ⅛"-diameter dowel painted brown
- 6" length fishing line
- Hot-glue gun

Instructions

1. Cut plastic canvas according to graphs. Cut one 20-hole x 13-hole piece for birdhouse bottom. Bottom will remain unstitched.

2. Stitch pieces following graphs. Using 6 strands floss, work embroidery on sides when background stitching is completed.

3. Overcast bird hole with camel, top edges of front, back and sides with eggshell and side and bottom edges of roof pieces with sail blue.

4. With eggshell, Whipstitch front and back to sides, then Whipstitch front, back and sides to bottom. With wrong sides together, Whipstitch top edges of roof pieces together with sail blue.

5. Thread fishing line through hole indicated on roof pieces. Tie ends to form a loop for hanging.

6. Using photo as a guide, glue bird hole to front, then glue dowel to front below bird hole. Center and glue roof to birdhouse.

—*Design by Vickie Baggett*

COLOR KEY	
Plastic Canvas Yarn	**Yards**
▨ Sail blue #04	11
☐ Eggshell #24	14
▨ Camel #34	1
6-Strand Embroidery Floss	
✎ Willow green #904 Backstitch	1
⌀ Willow green #904 Lazy Daisy	
⌀ Very dark dusty rose	
#3350 Lazy Daisy	1
○ Bright canary #973 French Knot	1
● Attach fishing line	
Color numbers given are for Darice Nylon Plus plastic canvas yarn and DMC 6-strand embroidery floss.	

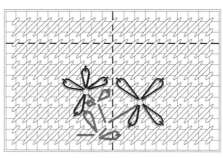

Mini Birdhouse Side
20 holes x 13 holes
Cut 2

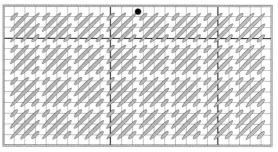

Mini Birdhouse Roof
25 holes x 13 holes
Cut 2

Top

Mini Birdhouse Bird Hole
5 holes x 5 holes
Cut 1

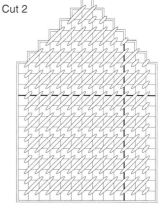

Mini Birdhouse Front & Back
13 holes x 19 holes
Cut 2

Milk Money Bank

If you're a mother with school-age children, you never have to hear, "Mom, I need milk money!" again! Just stitch this quick project and keep it stocked with spare change!

Skill Level: Beginner

Materials
- ½ sheet 7-count plastic canvas
- Worsted weight yarn as listed in color key
- 6-strand embroidery floss as listed in color key
- 1-pint canning jar with lid ring

COLOR KEY	
Worsted Weight Yarn	**Yards**
■ Black	1
□ White	4
6-Strand Embroidery Floss	
✂ Black Backstitch	1

Instructions

1. Cut plastic canvas according to graphs.

2. Stitch pieces following graphs, Overcasting tag edges and inside edges of lid with white.

3. Thread a 9½" length of white yarn through upper left hole of tag; tie around neck of jar, trimming ends as necessary.

4. Insert stitched lid piece in ring; screw onto jar.

—*Design by Debi Yorston*

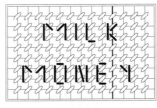

Bank Tag
14 holes x 9 holes
Cut 1

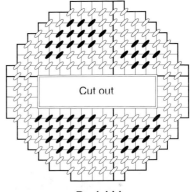

Cut out

Bank Lid
17 holes x 17 holes
Cut 1

Plant Pokes a-Plenty!

Plant pokes have dozens of delightful uses! Stitch the colorful Henny Hen and Bonny Bluebird plant pokes to cheer up a sick friend. Add an artistic touch to a silk arrangement in your own home with one or all three Metallic Expressions plant pokes. Liven up that spring bouquet in the kitchen with the pretty Simply a Strawberry poke. Whatever the occasion, plant pokes make great accents and work up in a jiffy!

Bonny Bluebird

Skill Level: Beginner

Materials

- ½ sheet 7-count Darice Ultra Stiff plastic canvas
- Red Heart Classic worsted weight yarn Art. E267 as listed in color key
- 6-strand embroidery floss as listed in color key
- 3 (1") pink silk flowers
- 8" ½"-wide pink floral ribbon
- 1¼"-diameter circle black Fun Foam craft foam by Westrim Crafts
- 1¾" x 1" strip white Fun Foam craft foam by Westrim Crafts
- 8" ¼"-diameter wooden dowel painted green
- Low-temperature glue gun

Instructions

1. Cut plastic canvas according to graphs (page 17).

2. Stitch pieces following graphs. Add black floss French Knot to bird when background stitching is completed. Overcast edges with adjacent colors.

3. Using photo as a guide through step 6, glue wing to bird, then glue bird to left side of birdhouse so bottom edge of bird rests on top edge of brown platform.

4. Glue leaves to right side of birdhouse and to platform. Place two flowers on birdhouse between leaves and one between roof and circular opening; attach with honey gold by coming up through center of flower, forming a French Knot and going down through center of flower.

5. Glue black craft foam behind circular opening.

Glue dowel to center back of birdhouse, allowing 6" below birdhouse. Secure by gluing strip of white craft foam to dowel and back of stitched piece.

6. Tie ½" ribbon in a bow, trimming tails as desired. Glue bow to dowel just under platform of birdhouse.

—Design by Celia Lange Designs

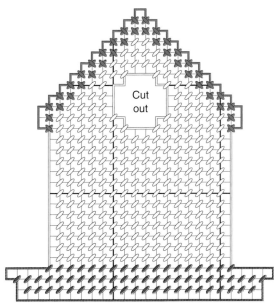

Bonny Bluebird Birdhouse
25 holes x 27 holes
Cut 1

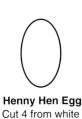

Henny Hen Egg
Cut 4 from white
craft foam

COLOR KEY	
BONNY BLUEBIRD	
Worsted Weight Yarn	**Yards**
☐ Eggshell #111	4
■ Mid brown #339	2
▨ Honey gold #645	1
■ Paddy green #686	3
▨ Light periwinkle #827	3
■ Periwinkle #831	1
6-Strand Embroidery Floss	
● Black French Knot	⅙
Color numbers given are for Red Heart Classic Art. E267 worsted weight yarn.	

Bonny Bluebird
17 holes x 10 holes
Cut 1

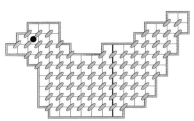

Bonny Bluebird Bottom Leaf
4 holes x 5 holes
Cut 1

Bonny Bluebird Wing
8 holes x 4 holes
Cut 1

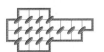

Bonny Bluebird Top Leaf
5 holes x 5 holes
Cut 1

Henny Hen

Skill Level: Beginner

Materials

- ½ sheet 7-count Darice Ultra Stiff plastic canvas
- Red Heart Classic worsted weight yarn Art. E267 as listed in color key
- Darice straw satin raffia cord as listed in color key
- 4mm round movable eye
- 8" ½"-wide yellow gingham ribbon
- Small amount white Fun Foam craft foam by Westrim Crafts
- 8" ¼"-diameter wooden dowel painted green
- Low-temperature glue gun

Instructions

1. Cut plastic canvas according to graphs (below and page 18). Following pattern given, cut four eggs from white craft foam.

2. Stitch pieces following graphs. Overcast pieces with adjacent colors.

3. Using photo as a guide through step 6, thread raffia from front to back where indicated along top of nest. Cut raffia, leaving strands ½"–1" long. Glue eggs to nest among strands of raffia.

4. Glue movable eye to head where indicated on graph. Glue nest to lower part of hen.

5. Cut a 2" x 1" strip white craft foam. Glue dowel to center back of hen, allowing 5½" below nest. Secure by gluing strip of white craft foam to dowel and back of stitched piece.

6. Tie ½" ribbon in a bow, trimming tails as desired. Center and glue bow to nest.

—Design by Celia Lange Designs

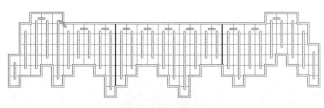

Henny Hen Nest
29 holes x 8 holes
Cut 1

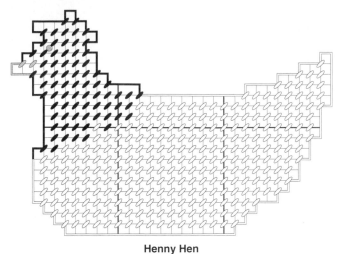

Henny Hen
30 holes x 21 holes
Cut 1

COLOR KEY	
HENNY HEN	
Worsted Weight Yarn	**Yards**
☐ White #1	5
■ Black #12	2
■ Honey gold #645	1
■ Cardinal #917	1
Straw Satin Raffia	
☐ Natural #3401-07	3
⁄ Attach raffia strands	
● Attach movable eye	

Color numbers given are for Red Heart Classic Art. E267 worsted weight yarn.

Simply a Strawberry

Skill Level: Beginner

Materials

- Small piece 10-count plastic canvas
- DMC 6-strand embroidery floss as listed in color key
- #22 tapestry needle
- Pink felt
- Wooden skewer
- Craft glue

Instructions

1. Cut plastic canvas according to graph. Cut felt to fit strawberry shape.

2. Continental Stitch and Overcast piece with 12 strands floss following graph. Work Backstitches with 3 strands off-white floss.

3. Apply glue to back of stitched piece. Center skewer on back and cover with felt. Press along edges firmly until glue begins to set.

—*Design by Kathleen Marie O'Donnell*

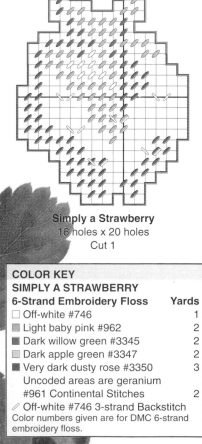

Simply a Strawberry
16 holes x 20 holes
Cut 1

COLOR KEY	
SIMPLY A STRAWBERRY	
6-Strand Embroidery Floss	**Yards**
☐ Off-white #746	1
■ Light baby pink #962	2
■ Dark willow green #3345	2
■ Dark apple green #3347	2
■ Very dark dusty rose #3350	3
Uncoded areas are geranium #961 Continental Stitches	2
⁄ Off-white #746 3-strand Backstitch	

Color numbers given are for DMC 6-strand embroidery floss.

Metallic Expressions

Skill Level: Beginner

Materials

Each Plant Poke

- Small amount 7-count plastic canvas
- Uniek Needloft metallic craft cord as listed in color key
- Beading needle and black sewing thread
- Bamboo skewer
- Hot-glue gun

Butterfly

- Uniek Needloft plastic canvas yarn as listed in color key
- 9 black giant seed beads
- Pair black flower stamens

Hummingbird

- Small black seed bead
- Hot-glue gun

Watermelon

- 7 black giant seed beads

Instructions

1. Cut plastic canvas according to graphs (page 24).

2. For butterfly, stitch with solid teal craft cord first following graph A. Following graph B, stitch solid gold craft cord over solid teal on upper wings. Overcast head with black yarn. Overcast upper wings with solid gold and bottom wings with solid teal.

3. For butterfly body, with beading needle and black thread, bring needle up through bottom center hole where indicated on graph B with blue dot. Thread on giant seed beads, then bring needle down through top center hole where indicated on graph B with blue dot. Secure beads at intervals down length of body by bringing needle up through center hole, over beading thread and down through same hole.

4. Glue stamens to back of head for antennae. Center and glue skewer to back of finished piece.

5. For hummingbird, stitch piece following graph. Overcast beak with black and remaining edges with adjacent colors.

6. With beading needle and black thread, attach seed bead for eye. Center and glue skewer to back of finished piece.

7. For watermelon, stitch piece following graph.

Overcast with adjacent colors.

8. Using photo as a guide, with beading needle and black thread, attach beads as desired to red area of watermelon. Glue skewer to back of finished piece.

—*Designs by Ruby Thacker*

Decorative Birdhouses

Stitch a trio of coordinating heart-shaped bird-houses. You'll find many occasions for sharing the plant poke, window ornament and magnet.

Skill Level: Intermediate

Materials
Each Birdhouse

- ¼ sheet 7-count plastic canvas

- 2 (3") Darice 7-count plastic canvas heart shapes
- Uniek Needloft plastic canvas yarn as listed in color key
- Tacky glue
- Hot-glue gun

Plant Poke

- 1 yard ⅛"-wide blue satin ribbon
- 2 (¾") minibirds
- Small ivy spray

- Assorted small pink and white flowers
- Small amount Spanish moss
- ³⁄₁₆"-diameter wooden dowel:
  1¼" length
  14" length

Ornament

- 1 yard ⅛"-wide gold ribbon
- ¾" minibird
- 4 large pink ribbon roses
- 4 tiny blue ribbon roses
- Filler flowers
- 9" white pearl string
- 25 (3mm) gold beads
- Small length florist wire
- 2" ³⁄₁₆"-diameter wooden dowel
- 22" gold lamé cord

Magnet

- 1 yard ⅛"-wide gold ribbon
- ¾" minibird
- 3 mauve rosebuds
- Small spray gold popcorn flowers or other filler
- 2" ³⁄₁₆"-diameter wooden dowel
- 2" magnetic strip

Cutting & Stitching

1. Cut birdhouse sides and holes on birdhouse fronts according to graphs (page 22).

2. Stitch plant poke sides, reversing one side before stitching; Overcast cutout area on short edges with dark royal. Stitch ornament sides as graphed. Stitch magnet sides replacing burgundy with forest.

3. Stitch ornament front and back following graphs. Stitch plant poke front and back replacing pink with sail blue. Stitch magnet front and back replacing pink with baby green. Overcast inside edges of front pieces with adjacent colors.

Plant Poke Assembly

1. Using dark royal throughout and with right sides together, Whipstitch short edges of sides without cutouts together. Bring sides down and with wrong sides together, Whipstitch short edges with cutouts together. *Note: Cutout area is for 14" dowel.* Whipstitch sides to front and back, easing stitches around curves.

2. Using photo as a guide through step 5, hot-glue

⅛" blue satin ribbon around unstitched portions of heart front and back. Make two small bows and glue one each to center top of heart front and back.

3. Place tacky glue on one end of 14" dowel and insert in bottom hole of sides, pushing up to inside top of birdhouse. Place glue on one end of 1¼" dowel and insert into bottom (perch) hole on front piece until end touches 14" dowel. Allow to dry.

4. Insert small amount of Spanish moss into top opening on front to cover dowel. Hot-glue small amounts of Spanish moss to top left of birdhouse and to bottom front under perch.

5. Glue one bird to perch and one to moss on top. Arrange flowers and ivy as desired in moss and glue in place.

Ornament Assembly

1. Using burgundy through step 2 and with right sides together, Whipstitch one short edge of each side together. Bring sides down and with wrong sides together, Whipstitch remaining short edges together. Whipstitch sides to front, easing stitches around curves.

2. Cut gold lamé cord in half. Place two lengths together and thread through center holes at top of ornament. Tie ends in a knot to form a loop for hanging. Whipstitch back to sides, easing stitches around curves.

3. Using photo as a guide through step 7, hot-glue ⅛" gold ribbon around unstitched portions of heart front and back. Make one small bow and glue to center top of heart back.

4. Place tacky glue on one end of 2" dowel and insert into bottom (perch) hole on front piece, pushing to back of birdhouse. Allow to dry.

5. Make three loops with pearl string and hot-glue under perch. Glue three large pink roses and three tiny blue roses among loops.

6. Making two sprays with eight beads and three sprays with three beads, place small amount of tacky glue on florist wire and insert into beads, leaving ½" wire below bottom bead. Allow to dry. Cut wire from tops of sprays. Hot-glue bead sprays and filler flowers as desired into floral arrangement.

7. Hot-glue one pink rose, one blue rose and small amount of filler flowers to center top of heart in front of hanging loop. Glue bird to perch.

Magnet Assembly

1. Using forest throughout and with right sides together, Whipstitch one short edge of each side together. Bring sides down and with wrong sides together, Whipstitch remaining short edges together. Whipstitch sides to front and back, easing stitches around curves.

2. Using photo as a guide through step 4, hot-glue ⅛" gold ribbon around unstitched portion of heart front. Make one small bow and glue to center top of heart front.

3. Place tacky glue on one end of 2" dowel and insert into bottom (perch) hole on front piece, pushing to back of birdhouse. Allow to dry.

4. Hot-glue bird to perch. Glue rosebuds and gold flowers as desired to bottom front. Glue magnetic strip to back.

—Designs by Ruby Thacker

Birdhouse Front
Cut 3
Stitch 1 as graphed for ornament
Stitch 1 for magnet, replacing pink with
baby green and burgundy with forest
Stitch 1 for plant poke, replacing pink with
sail blue and burgundy with dark royal

Birdhouse Ornament & Magnet Side
31 holes x 7 holes
Cut 4
Stitch 2 as graphed for ornament
Stitch 2 with forest for magnet

COLOR KEY	
Plastic Canvas Yarn	**Yards**
■ Burgundy #03	8
▨ Pink #07	7
Baby green #26	7
Forest #29	8
Sail blue #35	7
■ Dark royal #48	8
Color numbers given are for Uniek Needloft plastic canvas yarn.	

Birdhouse Back
Stitch 1 as graphed for ornament
Stitch 1 for magnet, replacing pink with
baby green and burgundy with forest
Stitch 1 for plant poke, replacing pink with
sail blue and burgundy with dark royal

Birdhouse Plant Poke Side
31 holes x 7 holes
Cut 2, reverse 1

Rainy-Day Gift-Bag Tags

Cheer up a friend with the blues by sending him or her a "thinking of you" gift embellished with an attractive umbrella gift-bag tag.

Skill Level: Beginner

Materials

- ⅓ sheet 10-count plastic canvas
- Anchor #3 pearl cotton by Coats & Clark as listed in color key
- Kreinik ⅛" Ribbon as listed in color key
- #22 tapestry needle
- 1 each pink and blue small ribbon roses
- Ivory-and-gold small ribbon rose
- 6" ¼"-wide pink braid trim
- 6" ¼"-wide ivory-and-gold braid trim
- 6" ⅛"-wide pink satin ribbon
- 6" ⅛"-wide ivory satin ribbon
- Glue or sewing needle and matching thread

Instructions

1. Cut plastic canvas according to graphs (page 24).

2. Stitch pieces following graphs, stitching "ribbing" first with Half Cross Stitches. Overcast umbrella A with navy pearl cotton and umbrella B with gold ribbon.

3. For umbrella A, stitch with sewing needle and matching thread or glue pink braid trim to umbrella where indicated on graph. Attach blue ribbon rose to center top of umbrella at top of braid trim.

4. Tie pink ribbon in a small bow, trimming ends as desired. Attach bow to handle where indicated on graph. Attach pink ribbon rose to center of bow.

5. For umbrella B, stitch with sewing needle and matching thread or glue ivory-and-gold braid trim to umbrella where indicated on graph. Attach ivory-and-gold ribbon rose to center top of umbrella at top of braid trim.

6. Tie ivory ¼" satin ribbon in a small bow, trimming ends as desired. Attach bow to handle where indicated on graph.

7. Attach as desired to gift bag.

—Designs by Carol Krob

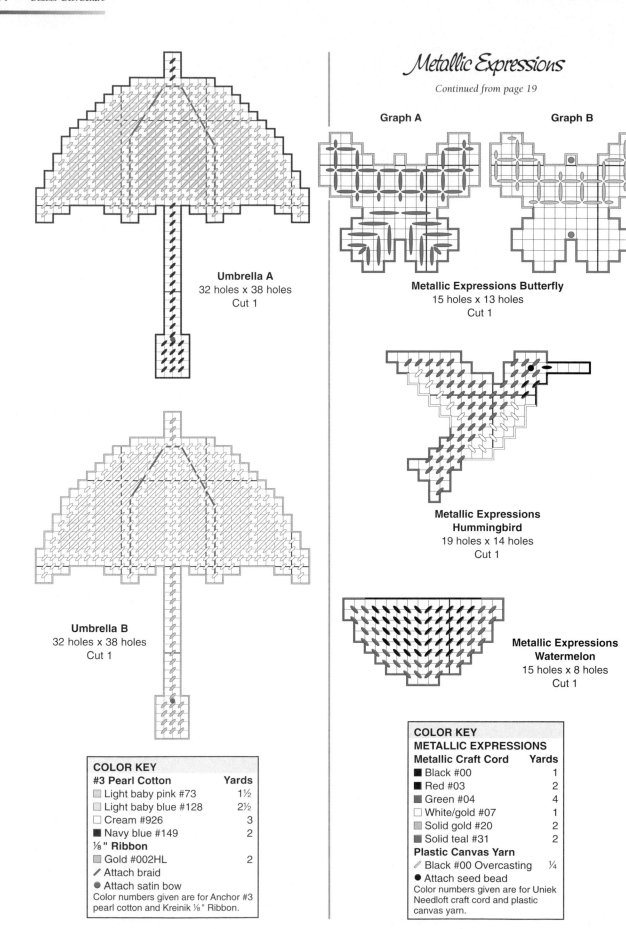

Metallic Expressions

Continued from page 19

Graph A

Graph B

Metallic Expressions Butterfly
15 holes x 13 holes
Cut 1

Umbrella A
32 holes x 38 holes
Cut 1

Metallic Expressions
Hummingbird
19 holes x 14 holes
Cut 1

Umbrella B
32 holes x 38 holes
Cut 1

Metallic Expressions
Watermelon
15 holes x 8 holes
Cut 1

COLOR KEY

#3 Pearl Cotton	Yards
Light baby pink #73	1½
Light baby blue #128	2½
Cream #926	3
Navy blue #149	2
⅛" Ribbon	
Gold #002HL	2
Attach braid	
Attach satin bow	

Color numbers given are for Anchor #3 pearl cotton and Kreinik ⅛" Ribbon.

COLOR KEY
METALLIC EXPRESSIONS

Metallic Craft Cord	Yards
Black #00	1
Red #03	2
Green #04	4
White/gold #07	1
Solid gold #20	2
Solid teal #31	2
Plastic Canvas Yarn	
Black #00 Overcasting	¼
Attach seed bead	

Color numbers given are for Uniek Needloft craft cord and plastic canvas yarn.

Quick-as-a-Wink Baskets

Rustic raffia ribbon gives these handy baskets a warm, country touch! These little baskets are perfect for filling with candy, dried flower petals or other favorite treasures!

Skill Level: Beginner

Materials
- 1 sheet 7-count plastic canvas
- 3" plastic canvas radial circle
- 4" plastic canvas radial circle
- Straw raffia as listed in color key
- #16 tapestry needle

Round Basket

1. Cut plastic canvas according to graphs (page 26). Cut off the two outermost rows of holes from 3" circle for basket bottom. Basket bottom will remain unstitched.

2. Stitch side and handle following graphs. Overcast long edges of handle and top edge of side. Whipstitch short edges of side together, then Whipstitch side to unstitched bottom.

3. Whipstitch short edges of handle to top edges of basket side, making sure to place one handle edge at basket seam.

4. Tie a bow around handle with 8" of raffia.

Hearth-Side Basket

1. Cut handle from plastic canvas according to graph (page 26). Four-inch circle will remain uncut.

2. Stitch handle and bottom following graphs. Overcast long edges of handle and outside edge of basket.

3. Whipstitch short edges of handle to basket where indicated on graph. To keep basket bent, work tacking stitches in center of circle where indicated on graph with blue lines.

4. Tie a bow around handle with 8" of raffia.

Rectangular Basket

1. Cut plastic canvas according to graphs (page 26). Cut one 18-hole x 9-hole piece for basket bottom. Basket bottom will remain unstitched.

2. Stitch sides and handle following graphs. Overcast long edges of handle and top edges of sides. Whipstitch sides together, then Whipstitch sides to bottom.

3. Whipstitch short edges of handle to center top edges of basket short sides. Tie a bow around handle with 8" of raffia.

—Designs by Cherie Marie Leck

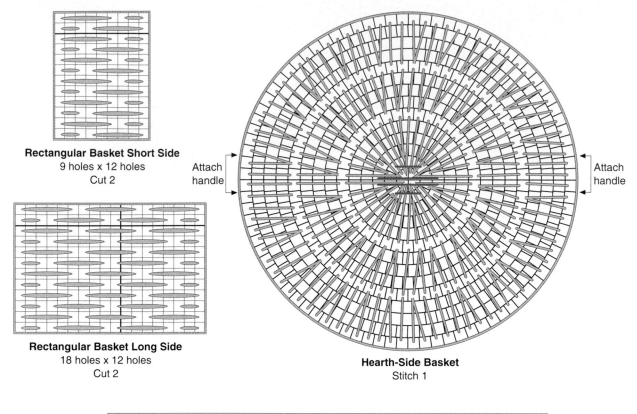

Rectangular Basket Short Side
9 holes x 12 holes
Cut 2

Rectangular Basket Long Side
18 holes x 12 holes
Cut 2

Attach
handle

Attach
handle

Hearth-Side Basket
Stitch 1

Hearth-Side Basket Handle
41 holes x 3 holes
Cut 1

Rectangular Basket Handle
36 holes x 3 holes
Cut 1

COLOR KEY	
Straw Raffia	**Ounces**
Natural	2

Round Basket Handle
37 holes x 3 holes
Cut 1

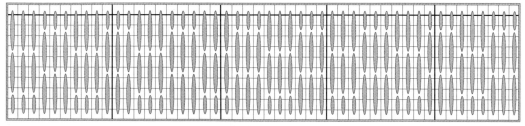

Round Basket Side
48 holes x 11 holes
Cut 1

Kitchen Geometry & An Apple a Day

Bright geometric shapes turn an everyday table setting into something special! Stitch a coordinating set, or use up your scrap yarn to make one of each for a fun kaleidoscope effect. Or, treat the young scholars in your family to an after-school snack, and encourage them to use a napkin by wrapping one up in a vibrant apple-shaped napkin ring.

Kitchen Geometry

Skill Level: Beginner

Materials
- ½ sheet 7-count plastic canvas
- Darice Nylon Plus plastic canvas yarn as listed in color key

Instructions
1. Cut and stitch plastic canvas according to graphs (page 28).

2. Overcast top and bottom edges with Christmas red. With yellow, Whipstitch short ends of each circle together, forming four napkin rings.

—*Designs by Nancy Marshall*

An Apple a Day

Skill Level: Beginner

Materials
- ⅓ sheet 7-count plastic canvas
- J. & P. Coats plastic canvas yarn Article E.46 as listed in color key

Instructions
1. Cut plastic canvas according to graph (page 28).

2. Stitch pieces, reversing one apple before stitching.

3. Whipstitch wrong sides of apples together using bright red for inside and outside edges of apple, medium brown for stem and paddy green for leaf.

—*Design by Nancy Marshall*

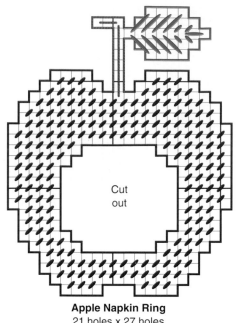

Apple Napkin Ring
21 holes x 27 holes
Cut 2, reverse 1

COLOR KEY

Plastic Canvas Yarn	Yards
■ Paddy green #686	1½
■ Bright red #901	7
✎ Medium brown #337	
Backstitch and Whipstitching	1

Color numbers given are for J. & P. Coats plastic canvas yarn Article E.46.

COLOR KEY
NAPKIN RING A

Plastic Canvas Yarn	Yards
■ Black #02	2
☐ Yellow #26	2
✎ Christmas red #19	
Overcasting	1½

Color numbers given are for Darice Nylon Plus plastic canvas yarn.

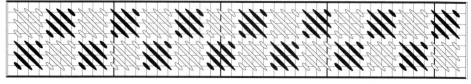

Napkin Ring A
43 holes x 7 holes
Cut 1

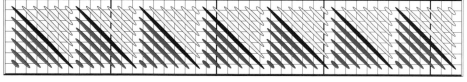

Napkin Ring B
43 holes x 7 holes
Cut 1

COLOR KEY
NAPKIN RING B

Plastic Canvas Yarn	Yards
■ Royal blue #09	1½
■ Christmas red #19	2
☐ Yellow #26	1½

Color numbers given are for Darice Nylon Plus plastic canvas yarn.

COLOR KEY
NAPKIN RING C

Plastic Canvas Yarn	Yards
☐ Yellow #26	2
■ Christmas green #58	2
✎ Christmas red #19 Overcasting	1½

Color numbers given are for Darice Nylon Plus plastic canvas yarn.

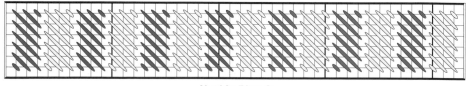

Napkin Ring C
43 holes x 7 holes
Cut 1

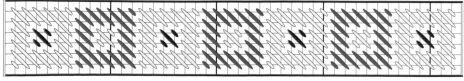

Napkin Ring D
43 holes x 7 holes
Cut 1

COLOR KEY
NAPKIN RING D

Plastic Canvas Yarn	Yards
■ Royal blue #09	1½
■ Christmas red #19	2
☐ Yellow #26	2

Color numbers given are for Darice Nylon Plus plastic canvas yarn.

Bon Voyage Luggage Tags

Stitch these easy-to-spot luggage tags for a friend who travels a lot, or even for attaching to a child's backpack. A combination of soft pastel colors and pretty design makes each tag appealing to people of all ages.

Skill Level: Beginner

Materials

- 1 sheet 7-count plastic canvas
- Plastic canvas yarn as listed in color key
- #16 tapestry needle
- 4 (3¾" x 2¼") pieces plastic sheeting
- 4 (3½ x 2") unlined index cards

Instructions

1. Cut and stitch plastic canvas according to graphs (pages 32 and 34).

2. Using light green throughout, Overcast inside edges and top edges of front and back of green tag. With wrong sides together, Whipstitch around sides and bottom.

3. Repeat step 2 for remaining tags, using cream yarn for roses tag, denim yarn for blue tag and lavender yarn for lavender tag.

4. Write address on index cards. Place plastic sheeting and address card inside each tag.

—*Designs by Elayne Tunnell*

Green Tag Back
17 holes x 31 holes
Cut 1

Green Tag Front
17 holes x 31 holes
Cut 1

COLOR KEY	
GREEN TAG	
Plastic Canvas Yarn	**Yards**
☐ Light green	12
☐ Cream	10

Lavender Tag Back
16 holes x 28 holes
Cut 1

COLOR KEY	
ROSES TAG	
Plastic Canvas Yarn	**Yards**
☐ Cream	10
☐ Dark pink	5
☐ Green	4

COLOR KEY	
LAVENDER TAG	
Plastic Canvas Yarn	**Yards**
☐ Lavender	6
☐ Light lavender	4

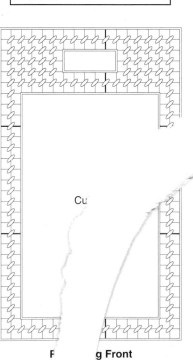

R___ ___g Front
___ 29 holes
___t 1

Roses Tag Back
17 holes x 29 holes
Cut 1

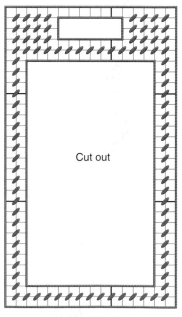

Lavender Tag Front
16 holes x 28 holes
Cut 1

Traffic Light Key Chain

This eye-catching key chain holder is easy to find, thus making it harder to misplace your keys! It holds coins, too!

Skill Level: Intermediate

Materials

- ½ sheet Uniek Quick-Count 7-count plastic canvas
- Uniek Needloft plastic canvas yarn as listed in color key
- DMC #3 pearl cotton as listed in color key
- #16 tapestry needle
- 4" gold ball link key chain
- Hot-glue gun

Instructions

1. Cut plastic canvas according to graphs (page 34). Cut three 15-hole x 2-hole pieces for light shades.

2. Continental Stitch key chain back and light shades with straw. Stitch front following graph, Continental Stitching uncoded area with straw. Backstitch key chain front with black pearl cotton over completed Continental Stitching.

3. Overcast light shades and slit opening on key chain back with straw. Tack one light shade above each light on front from blue dot to blue dot, taking stitches as necessary to hold curve.

4. Apply lines of glue on wrong side of back where indicated on graph. Place wrong side of key chain front on back. Allow to dry.

5. With straw, Whipstitch key chain front and back together along outside edges and at key chain opening.

6. Insert key chain through opening. Insert quarters into slots in back.

—Design by Vicki Blizzard

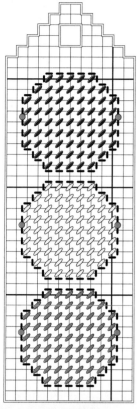

Key Chain Front
12 holes x 37 holes
Cut 1

Bon Voyage Luggage Tags

Continued from page 32

COLOR KEY		
BLUE TAG		
Plastic Canvas Yarn		**Yards**
■ Dark blue		2
■ Denim		12
□ Blue		1
□ Light blue		4

COLOR KEY	
Plastic Canvas Yarn	**Yards**
■ Christmas red #02	1½
■ Christmas green #28	1½
□ Yellow #58	1½
Uncoded areas are straw #19 Continental Stitches	14
⁄ Straw #14 Overcasting and Whipstitching	
#3 Pearl Cotton	
╱ Black #310 Backstitch	2
— Apply glue	
Color numbers given are for Uniek Needloft plastic canvas yarn and DMC #3 pearl cotton.	

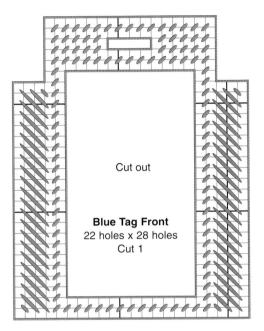

Cut out

Blue Tag Front
22 holes x 28 holes
Cut 1

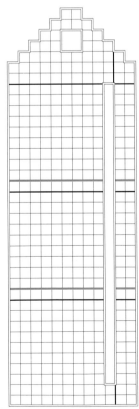

Key Chain Back
12 holes x 37 holes
Cut 1

Blue Tag Back
22 holes x 28 holes
Cut 1

Easy Home Accents

With today's woman busier than ever, you need projects you can make in little time. And why not start with projects for the home? Whether you need to stitch a quick table set for the newlyweds or a set of pretty coasters for yourself, you'll find many delightful ideas in this chapter.

Strawberry Hostess Set

Delight a group of friends by serving up a light lunch on this lovely luncheon set! Luscious strawberries and eyelet lace make just the right combination on a navy blue background.

Skill Level: Beginner

Materials

- 7-count plastic canvas place mat oval
- 1 sheet 7-count plastic canvas
- Uniek Needloft plastic canvas yarn as listed in color key
- Kreinik Medium (#16) Braid as listed in color key
- #16 tapestry needle
- 1½ yards 1"-wide white pre-gathered eyelet lace
- ½ yard lining fabric and matching sewing thread (optional)
- Hot-glue gun

Instructions

1. Cut plastic canvas according to graphs. Do not cut oval place mat.

2. Using dark royal throughout, stitch place mat oval in vertical Slanting Gobelin Stitches over three bars, compensating around curves as necessary. Overcast place mat edges.

3. Stitch remaining pieces following graphs, revers-

ing four strawberry caps before stitching. Use 1 ply white yarn to stitch and Overcast flowers. Work French Knots in flower centers when background stitching and Overcasting are completed. For seeds, work five-star yellow braid French Knots where desired on each strawberry.

4. Overcast strawberries, strawberry caps and leaves with adjacent colors. Using dark royal throughout, Overcast top edges of pocket front and back. With wrong sides together, Whipstitch pocket front and back together around side and bottom edges.

5. Glue lace to back of place mat around edges and to inside top edges of pocket. Glue caps to top of strawberries. Using photo as a guide, arrange berries, leaves and flowers as desired on left side of place mat and on pocket front; glue in place.

6. If desired, cut lining fabric ¼" larger all around than place mat oval. Fold ¼" to inside and press in place. Sew lining to back of place mat with matching thread, covering glued lace.

—*Design by Vicki Blizzard*

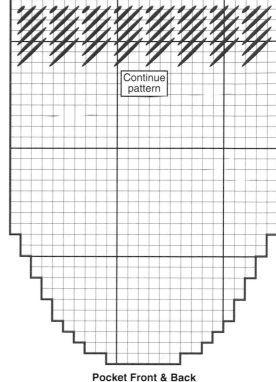

Pocket Front & Back
25 holes x 34 holes
Cut 2

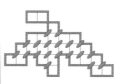

Strawberry Cap
10 holes x 6 holes
Cut 8, reverse 4

Flower
3 holes x 3 holes
Cut 14

Leaf
7 holes x 10 holes
Cut 7

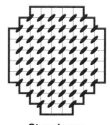

Strawberry
9 holes x 10 holes
Cut 8

COLOR KEY

Plastic Canvas Yarn	Yards
■ Christmas red #02	16
▨ Fern #23	15
☐ White #41	3
■ Dark royal #48	92
Medium (#16) Braid	
○ Star yellow #091 French Knot	4

Color numbers given are for Uniek Needloft plastic canvas yarn and Kreinik Medium (#16) Braid.

Bath Time

Add a hand-stitched accent to your bathroom with this delightful wall hanging. Guests as well as family members will love its old-time charm!

Skill Level: Beginner

Materials

- 1 sheet Darice Ultra Stiff 7-count plastic canvas
- Red Heart Classic Art. E267 worsted weight yarn as listed in color key
- DMC #3 pearl cotton as listed in color key
- Natural raffia
- 10 (5mm) iridescent beads
- Scraps of sponge
- 2" square of towel with fringe
- White paper
- 1" x ⅝" piece cardboard
- Glue stick or white glue
- Low-temperature glue gun

Instructions

1. Cut plastic canvas according to graphs.

2. Stitch and Overcast pieces following graphs. Work embroidery with #3 pearl cotton.

3. Braid raffia into a 22"-long piece including 1" fringe and knot at top and 3" fringe and knot at bottom. Tie a few strands raffia into a 4½" bow. Glue bow to knot at top of braid.

4. Trace or copy privy sign (Fig. 1) on white paper; glue to cardboard using glue stick or white glue. Cut sponge into one ⅝" x ⅜" x ³⁄₁₆"-deep piece for tub and one ⅞" x ½" x ⅜"-deep piece for bow center. Fold and glue side edges of towel under so towel is 1¾" wide. Trim fringe to proportional length.

5. Using photo as a guide and low-temperature glue gun through step 8, glue roof to top of outhouse and door to center front of outhouse. Glue privy sign above door.

6. Glue tub rim to top edge of tub. Glue tub sponge to left side of rim. Glue two beads to top edge of tub and rim on right side and three beads to top edge of tub and rim on left side just next to the sponge.

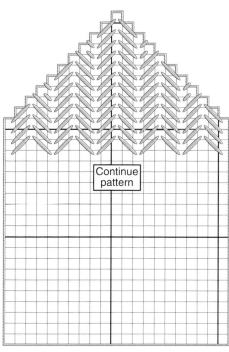

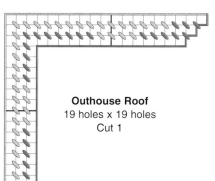

Outhouse Roof
19 holes x 19 holes
Cut 1

Outhouse Door
7 holes x 14 holes
Cut 1

Fig. 1

PRIVY

Outhouse
21 holes x 31 holes
Cut 1

COLOR KEY	
Worsted Weight Yarn	**Yards**
☐ White #1	6
■ Black #12	1
☐ Tan #334	8
☐ Light seafoam #683	3
■ Seafoam #684	3
☐ Pale blue #815	1
Uncoded areas are off-white	
#3 Continental Stitches	4
#3 Pearl Cotton	
✦ Black #310 Straight Stitch	⅙
✦ Medium beige brown	
#840 Backstitch	1
✦ Dark blue green #991 Backstitch	1
Color numbers given are for Red Heart Classic Art. E267 worsted weight yarn and DMC #3 pearl cotton.	

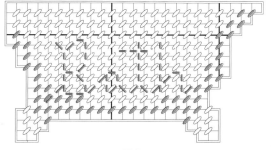

Soap
22 holes x 11 holes
Cut 1

Tub
24 holes x 13 holes
Cut 1

7. Glue three beads to top right front of soap sign and two to bottom left front of soap sign.

8. Gather and glue top edge of towel just under raffia bow center; glue remaining sponge to center of bow so that it covers top edge of towel. Center and glue outhouse approximately ¾" below towel. Center and glue tub and soap under outhouse 1¾"–2" apart.

9. Hang as desired.

—Design by Celia Lange Designs

Tub Rim
26 holes x 3 holes
Cut 1

Cheery Flower Frames

Frame the sweetest flowers in your life in this set of bright frames.
They're just the right size for framing wallet-size school photos.

Skill Level: Intermediate

Materials

- ½ sheet 10-count plastic canvas
- DMC #3 pearl cotton as listed in color key
- 6 (½") square magnet strips
- White felt (optional)
- Hot-glue gun

Instructions

1. Cut plastic canvas according to graphs (right and page 41).

2. Continental Stitch pieces following graphs. Overcast outer edges of all three frames with white.

3. Overcast inside edges of frame A with bright canary. Overcast frame A bow center with very dark violet. Overcast frame A bow with very dark violet and light lavender following graph.

4. Overcast inside edges of frame B with Christmas gold and deep orchid following graph. Overcast frame B leaf with light Nile green.

Frame C Leaf
10 holes x 27 holes
Cut 1

5. Overcast inside edges of frame C with topaz. Overcast frame C leaf with light Nile green and bright Christmas green following graph.

6. Using photo as a guide through step 7, for frame A, wrap bow center around bow and glue in place on backside of bow; glue or sew bow and bow center to frame A where indicated on graph.

7. Sew or glue corresponding leaves to frames B and C where indicated on graphs.

8. Glue or tape photos in place. If desired, cut felt to fit backs of frames and glue in place. Glue two magnet strips to back of each frame.

—*Designs by Judi Kauffman*

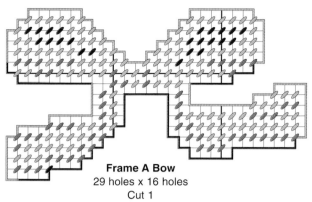

Frame A Bow
29 holes x 16 holes
Cut 1

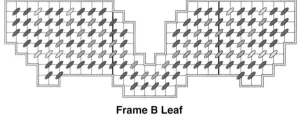

Frame B Leaf
27 holes x 9 holes
Cut 1

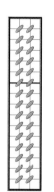

Frame A Bow Center
3 holes x 16 holes
Cut 1

COLOR KEY

#3 Pearl Cotton	Yards
Light lavender #210	2
Bright canary #307	1
Very dark violet #550	2
Light violet #553	2
Medium cranberry #603	2
Very light cranberry #605	1½
Bright Christmas green #700	3
Bright chartreuse #703	2
Deep orchid #718	1
Topaz #725	1
Light Nile green #955	2
Christmas gold #972	1
Uncoded areas are white Continental Stitches	11

⁄ White Overcasting
● Attach bow
● Attach leaf
Color numbers given are for DMC #3 pearl cotton.

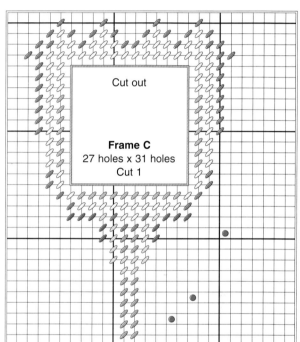

Cut out

Frame C
27 holes x 31 holes
Cut 1

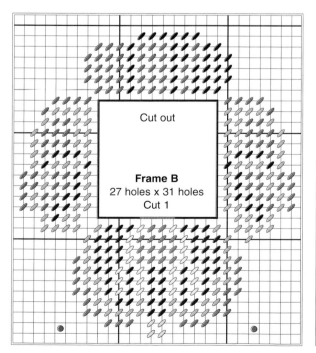

Cut out

Frame B
27 holes x 31 holes
Cut 1

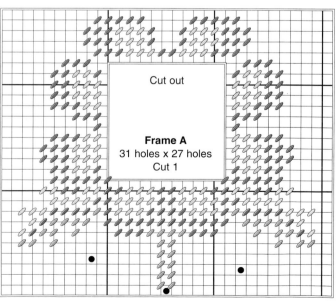

Cut out

Frame A
31 holes x 27 holes
Cut 1

Kitchen Piggies

Here's the perfect gift to stitch for a friend who collects pigs! A handy erasable message board and sweetener caddy will make her feel like she's in hog heaven!

Skill Level: Advanced

Message Board

Materials

- 2 sheets Darice Ultra Stiff 7-count plastic canvas
- ¼ sheet Darice Super Soft 7-count plastic canvas
- Red Heart Classic Art. E267 worsted weight yarn as listed in color key
- 9" x 12" piece white poster board
- 9" x 12" piece Con-Tact Brand MemoBoard self-adhesive write-and-wipe paper
- Dry-erase marker pen
- 2 sawtooth hangers
- Sewing needle and thread
- Low-temperature glue gun

Project Note

To change the shape of soft plastic canvas, bend and hold piece as desired with yarn. Heat-set by bringing needed amount of water to a boil. Remove water from heat source and place formed plastic canvas piece in water until water is cool to the touch. Dry plastic canvas and remove yarn.

Instructions

1. Cut head, snout and body front and back from stiff plastic canvas; cut tail from soft plastic canvas according to graphs (pages 44–46). Cut body front and body back as one piece, making sure not to repeat center line. Cut out opening on body front only. Body back will remain unstitched.

2. To curl tip of tail, thread a scrap length of yarn through holes indicated with blue dots on graph.

Pull yarn together until tip of tail is about ½" from main part of tail. Heat-set following project note.

3. Stitch body front following graphs and Fig. 1, making sure not to repeat center line. Intersections with green dots should not be stitched at this time. Work cameo rose Backstitches when background stitching is completed. Overcast inside edges with lily pink.

4. Stitch head, snout and tail following graphs, leaving intersections indicated with green dots on tail unstitched. When stitching tail, keep backside as neat as possible. Work Backstitches and Straight Stitches when background stitching is completed.

5. Overcast head, snout and tail following graphs. With lily pink and with tip of tail at the top, Whipstitch tail to body front where indicated with green dots, curling tail while attaching.

6. To make message board, cut poster board ½" larger all around than opening on body front. Apply self-adhesive write-and-wipe paper to poster board, following manufacturer's directions. Trim paper to size of poster board.

7. With sewing needle and thread, attach sawtooth hanger to top backside of unstitched body back, making sure hangers are placed on a horizontal straight line.

8. With message board between and with wrong sides together, Whipstitch body front to body back with cameo rose and off-white, following graph.

9. Using photo as a guide, glue snout to head and head to upper left body front. Place marker pen in curled tail.

Sweetener Caddy

Materials

- 1 sheet 7-count plastic canvas
- Red Heart Classic Art. E267 worsted weight yarn as listed in color key
- 3½" ⁵⁄₃₂"-wide porcelain pink bendable ribbon
- ³⁄₁₆"-diameter wooden dowel or size 8 knitting needle
- Low-temperature glue gun

Instructions

1. Cut plastic canvas according to graphs (also see page 46). Cut one 21-hole x 11-hole piece for caddy bottom. Bottom will remain unstitched.

2. Stitch pieces following graphs, leaving areas indicated with blue line on body sides unstitched.

Stitch head front as graphed and head back with lily pink Continental Stitches only.

3. Work embroidery when background stitching is completed, using 4 plies for cameo rose and cardinal Backstitching and 2 plies for white Straight Stitches and cameo rose French Knots.

4. Insert porcelain pink ribbon from front to back through hole indicated on body back graph; glue 1¼" of ribbon to backside. Trim remaining end at an angle and wrap ribbon tightly around dowel or knitting needle. Remove dowel and arrange curly tail as desired.

5. Overcast snout with cameo rose. Using lily pink through step 6, Overcast top edges of body front and back and top edges of body sides from dot to dot. Whipstitch wrong sides of head front and back together.

6. Whipstitch body front to body sides where indicated on side graphs, then continue up front edges of body sides. Whipstitch body back to back edges of body sides.

7. Following graph, Whipstitch body bottom to bottom edges of body front, back and sides; Overcast remaining edges of sides.

8. Using photo as a guide, glue snout to head front, then glue head to top left corner of body side A.

—Designs by Darla J. Fanton

Caddy Snout
4 holes x 4 holes
Cut 1

Caddy Body Side A
31 holes x 19 holes
Cut 1

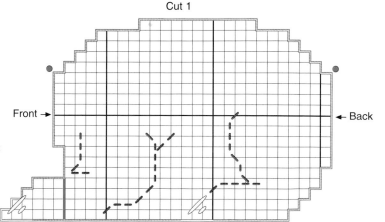

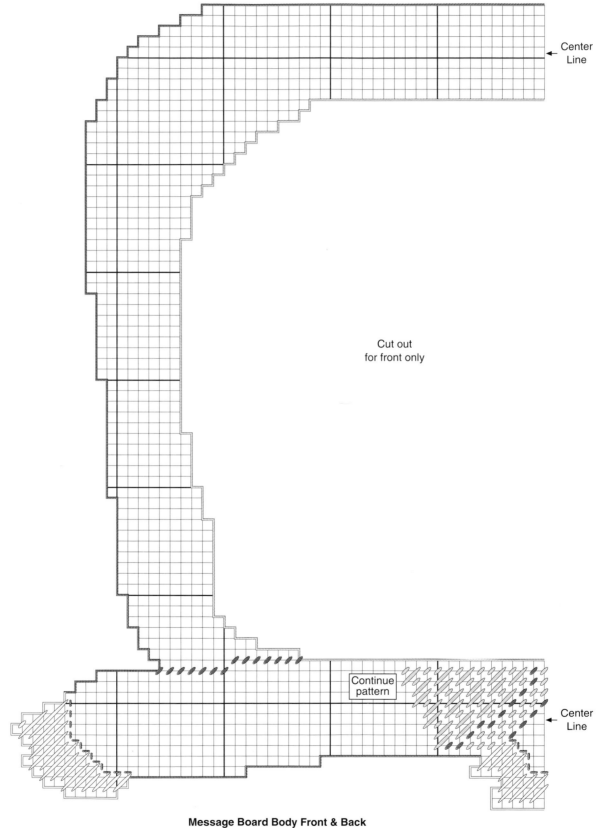

← Center Line

Cut out
for front only

Continue
pattern

← Center Line

Message Board Body Front & Back
100 holes x 75 holes
Cut 2, stitch 1, from stiff
*The two body front and back graphs
represent one piece of canvas. Cut
and work as one piece, being
careful not to repeat center line.*

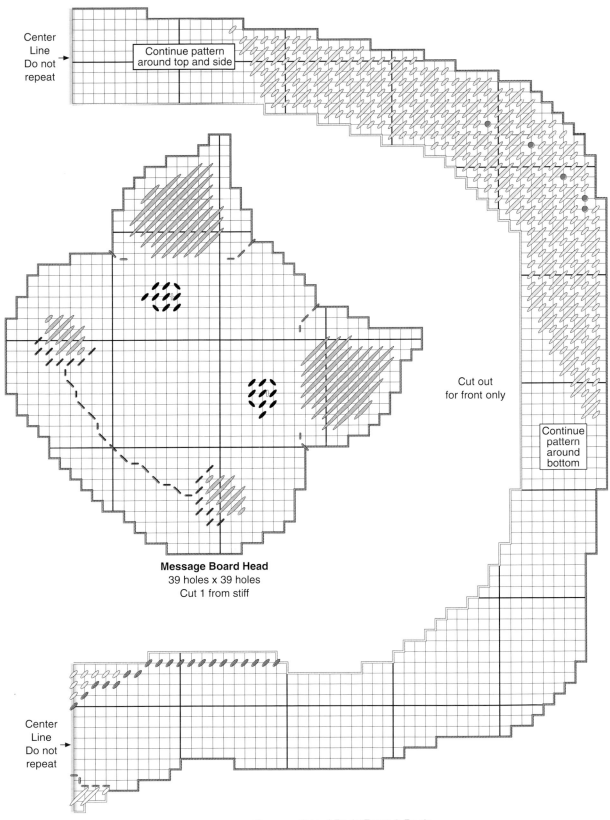

Center
Line
Do not
repeat

Continue pattern
around top and side

Cut out
for front only

Continue
pattern
around
bottom

Message Board Head
39 holes x 39 holes
Cut 1 from stiff

Center
Line
Do not
repeat

Message Board Body Front & Back
100 holes x 75 holes
Cut 2, stitch 1, from stiff
*The two body front and back graphs
represent one piece of canvas. Cut
and work as one piece, being
careful not to repeat center line.*

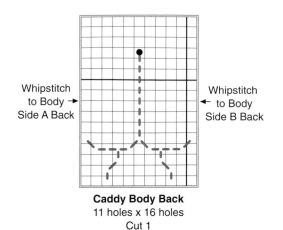

Whipstitch to Body Side A Back →

← Whipstitch to Body Side B Back

Caddy Body Back
11 holes x 16 holes
Cut 1

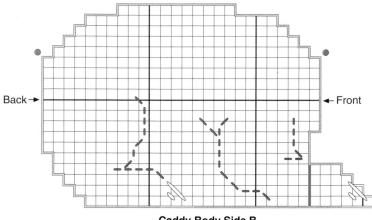

Back →

← Front

Caddy Body Side B
31 holes x 19 holes
Cut 1

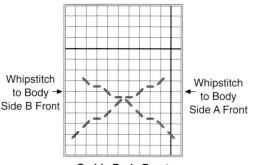

Whipstitch to Body Side B Front →

← Whipstitch to Body Side A Front

Caddy Body Front
11 holes x 14 holes
Cut 1

Cashmere Stitch
Bring needle up at 1, down at 2,
up at 3, down at 4, etc.

COLOR KEY
SWEETENER CADDY

Worsted Weight Yarn	Yards
☐ Off-white #3	2
■ Black #12	1
☐ Lily pink #719	25
▨ Pale rose #755	1
▨ Cameo rose #759	2

Uncoded areas are lily pink #719
Continental Stitches
⟋ White #1 2-ply Straight Stitch
⟋ Cameo rose #759 Backstitch
⟋ Cardinal #917 Backstitch 1
● Cameo rose #759 2-ply French Knot
● Attach ribbon tail
❘ Attach to body front
Color numbers given are for Red Heart Classic Art.
E267 worsted weight yarn.

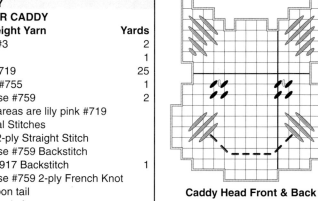

Caddy Head Front & Back
15 holes x 17 holes
Cut 2
Stitch 1 as graphed
Stitch 1 with pale pink
Continental Stitches only

COLOR KEY
MESSAGE BOARD

Plastic Canvas Yarn	Yards
☐ Off-white #3	3
■ Black #12	1
☐ Lily pink #719	45
▨ Pale rose #755	2
▨ Cameo rose #759	10
■ Cardinal #917	1

Uncoded areas are lily pink
#719 Continental Stitches
⟋ White #1 Straight Stitch 1
⟋ Cameo rose #759 Backstitch
⟋ Cardinal #917 Backstitch
Color numbers given are for Red Heart Classic
Art. E267 worsted weight yarn.

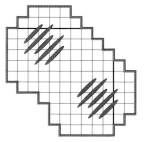

Message Board Snout
12 holes x 12 holes
Cut 1 from stiff

Message Board Tail
49 holes x 3 holes
Cut 1 from soft

Floral Napkin Rings

Stitched with a rainbow of colors, these enchanting napkin rings are as pretty as a bouquet!

Skill Level: Intermediate

Materials

- ½ sheet 10-count plastic canvas
- DMC #3 pearl cotton as listed in color key
- DMC 6-strand embroidery floss as listed in color key
- 4 (2" x 6½") pieces ecru felt
- Sewing needle and ecru sewing thread
- Hot-glue gun

Instructions

1. Cut plastic canvas according to graphs (pages 48 and 51). Cut a 6¼" x 1⅝" piece of felt lining for each napkin ring.

2. Leaving overlapped ends of Blue Flowers napkin ring unstitched for now, stitch remaining portion of ring following graph. Work Backstitches with 4 strands embroidery floss.

3. Overlap four unstitched holes on napkin ring ends and complete stitching following graph. Overcast top and bottom edges with ecru.

4. Fit one piece felt along backside of stitched napkin ring, overlapping ends of felt where plastic canvas is overlapped. Using sewing needle and ecru thread, attach felt to napkin ring along top and bottom rows of holes. Tack felt down along felt overlap.

5. Repeat steps 2–4 for each remaining napkin ring. Backstitch with 4 strands embroidery floss on all napkin rings and with pearl cotton on Peach Flowers napkin ring.

—Designs by Kathleen Marie O'Donnell

COLOR KEY ROSE FLOWERS	
#3 Pearl Cotton	**Yards**
☐ Ecru	10
■ Dark carnation #601	1
▨ Light cranberry #603	1
☐ Very light cranberry #605	1
☐ Deep canary #725	1
■ Very dark garnet #902	2
▨ Dark willow green #3345	2
☐ Dark apple green #3347	1
Uncoded areas are ecru	
Continental Stitches	
6-Strand Embroidery Floss	
╱ Very dark garnet #902	
4-strand Backstitch	

Color numbers given are for DMC #3 pearl cotton and 6-strand embroidery floss.

COLOR KEY PEACH FLOWERS	
#3 Pearl Cotton	**Yards**
☐ Ecru	10
■ Coral #351	1
▨ Peach flesh #352	1
☐ Light peach flesh #353	1
▨ Very dark garnet #902	3
■ Dark willow green #3345	1½
☐ Dark apple green #3347	1
Uncoded areas are ecru	
Continental Stitches	
╱ Deep canary #725 Backstitch	⅓
6-Strand Embroidery Floss	
╱ Very dark garnet #902	
4-strand Backstitch	

Color numbers given are for DMC #3 pearl cotton and 6-strand embroidery floss.

COLOR KEY PURPLE FLOWERS	
#3 Pearl Cotton	**Yards**
☐ Ecru	10
■ Medium lavender #208	2
▨ Light lavender #210	2
■ Medium violet #552	2
☐ Deep canary #725	½
■ Dark willow green #3345	1½
☐ Dark apple green #3347	1
Uncoded areas are ecru	
Continental Stitches	
6-Strand Embroidery Floss	
╱ Very dark navy blue #823	
4-strand Backstitch	3

Color numbers given are for DMC #3 pearl cotton and 6-strand embroidery floss.

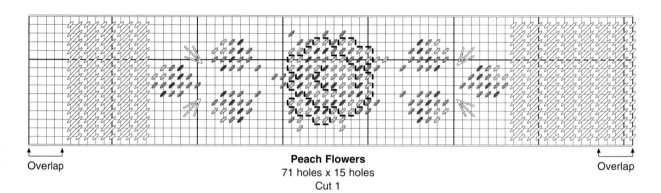

Overlap

Peach Flowers
71 holes x 15 holes
Cut 1

Overlap

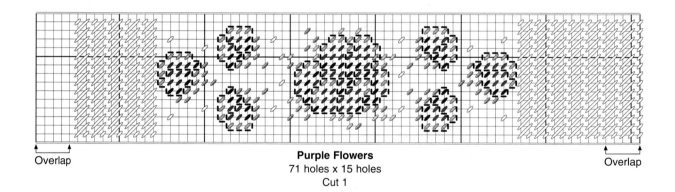

Overlap

Purple Flowers
71 holes x 15 holes
Cut 1

Overlap

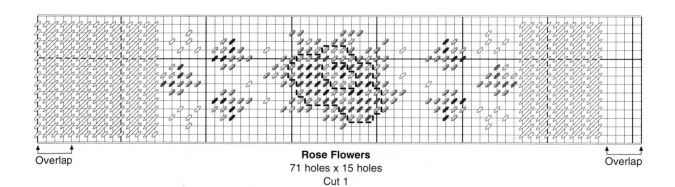

Overlap

Rose Flowers
71 holes x 15 holes
Cut 1

Overlap

Kitten Doorstop

Prop open a door with this cuddly-kitten-curled-up-in-a-slipper doorstop. She's so cute, you can almost hear her purring!

Skill Level: Intermediate

Materials
- 1 sheet 7-count plastic canvas
- Red Heart Classic Art. E267 worsted weight yarn as listed in color key
- Red Heart Classic Art. E267S sparkling worsted weight yarn as listed in color key
- DMC #3 pearl cotton as listed in color key
- Polyester fiberfill
- Clean, smooth pebbles or weight of choice
- Hot-glue gun

Instructions

1. Cut plastic canvas according to graphs (pages 50 and 51).

2. Stitch pieces following graphs, reversing one ear, one body and one slipper side before stitching. Following graphs, Overcast tail, head, paws and ears, Whipstitching dart at bottom of ears together to cup slightly. Backstitch face and paws when background stitching and Overcasting are completed.

3. Using cameo rose throughout, Whipstitch heels of slipper sides to slipper back. Whipstitch slipper front to toes of slipper sides, then Whipstitch top edges of slipper sides together from dot to dot. Overcast remaining top edges of sides and back.

4. Using nickel throughout and with wrong sides

together, Whipstitch body pieces together from dot to dot across top. Overcast remaining edges.

5. Using photo as a guide through step 6, stuff kitten body with fiberfill then position in slipper opening so that approximately the first eight rows of stitches show and the right edge is next to heel. Slip tail into slipper on left side of body; glue body and tail in place.

6. Glue head to top front of body. Position and glue paws to body, slipper front and bottom of head. Glue ears to backside of head.

7. Fill slipper with pebbles or desired weight. Whipstitch slipper bottom to slipper sides, front and back with new berry.

—*Design by Celia Lange Designs*

COLOR KEY	
Worsted Weight Yarn	**Yards**
☐ Sparkling white #100	4
▨ Nickel #401	10
▨ Pale rose #755	5
■ New berry #760	6
Uncoded areas are cameo rose #759 Continental Stitches	25
╱ Cameo rose #759 Overcasting and Whipstitching	
#3 Pearl Cotton	
╱ Black #310 Backstitch	1
Color numbers given are for Red Heart Classic Art. E267 and Art. E267S worsted weight yarn and DMC #3 pearl cotton.	

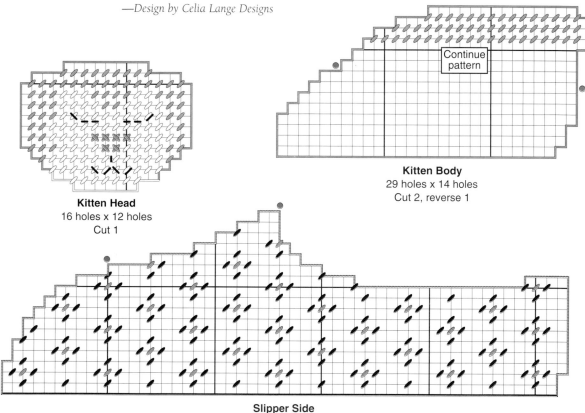

Kitten Head
16 holes x 12 holes
Cut 1

Kitten Body
29 holes x 14 holes
Cut 2, reverse 1

Slipper Side
53 holes x 17 holes
Cut 2, reverse 1

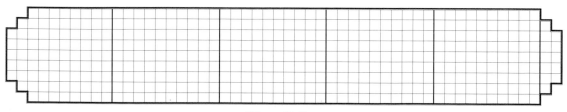

Slipper Bottom
52 holes x 9 holes
Cut 1

Kitten Paw A
10 holes x 7 holes
Cut 1

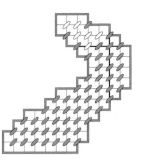

Kitten Tail
12 holes x 13 holes
Cut 1

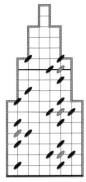

Slipper Front
7 holes x 16 holes
Cut 1

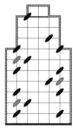

Slipper Back
6 holes x 11 holes
Cut 1

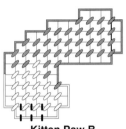

Kitten Paw B
11 holes x 10 holes
Cut 1

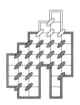

Kitten Ear
6 holes x 8 holes
Cut 2, reverse 1

COLOR KEY	
BLUE FLOWERS	
#3 Pearl Cotton	**Yards**
☐ Ecru	10
☐ Deep canary #725	1
▊ Dark cornflower blue #798	1
▨ Blue #799	1
☐ Baby blue #3325	1
▨ Dark willow green #3345	1
▨ Dark apple green #3347	1
Uncoded areas are ecru	
Continental Stitches	
6-Strand Embroidery Floss	
✎ Very dark navy blue #823 4-strand	
Backstitch and Straight Stitch	2½
Color numbers given are for DMC #3 pearl cotton and 6-strand embroidery floss.	

Floral Napkin Rings

Continued from page 48

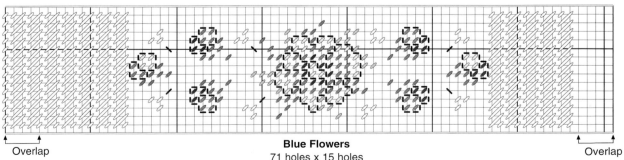

Overlap

Blue Flowers
71 holes x 15 holes
Cut 1

Overlap

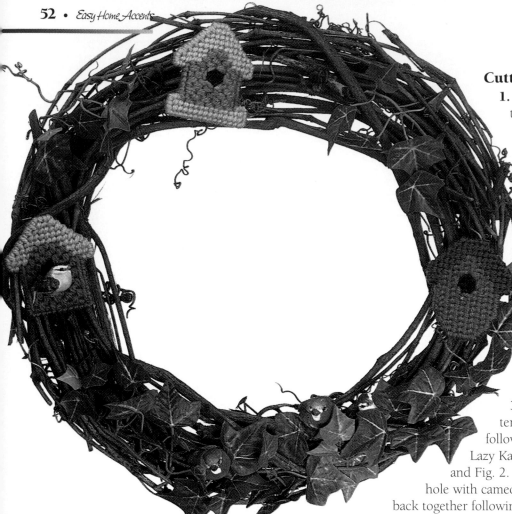

Birdhouse Wreath

Add a touch of country charm to your home with a quaint birdhouse wreath! In all shapes and sizes, each birdhouse is quick to stitch. Just glue them onto a grapevine wreath, add a bit of ivy, and voilá!—an easy home accent!

Skill Level: Beginner

Materials

- ½ sheet 7-count plastic canvas
- J. & P. Coats plastic canvas yarn Article E.46 as listed in color key
- #16 tapestry needle
- 14" grapevine wreath
- 3 (10"-long) ivy vine sprigs
- 4 mushroom birds
- Wooden toothpicks:
  1 pink
  2 blue green
- Glue gun

Cutting & Stitching

1. Cut plastic canvas according to graphs. Birdhouse backs will remain unstitched.

2. Continental Stitch roof, base and center hole of birdhouse A front following graphs. Stitch house with Horizontal Brick Stitches using two strands blue gray yarn, following graph and Fig. 1. Backstitch around center hole and along top of base with one strand blue gray yarn. Whipstitch front and back together following graph.

3. Cross Stitch roof and center hole of birdhouse B front following graph. Stitch house with Lazy Kalem Stitches following graph and Fig. 2. Backstitch around center hole with cameo rose. Whipstitch front and back together following graph.

4. Continental Stitch roof and center hole of birdhouse C following graph. Stitch house with Horizontal Brick Stitches using two strands seafoam following graph and Fig. 3. Work Straight Stitches with one strand seafoam. Whipstitch front and back together following graph.

Assembly

1. Cut 1" off each toothpick. Use blue green toothpicks for birdhouses A and C and pink toothpick for birdhouse B. Insert pointed ends of 1" pieces into fronts just under center holes, pushing through to back of canvas.

2. Using photo as a guide through step 4, glue birdhouses to wreath front. Forming one long strand, glue two sprigs ivy to center bottom of wreath, overlapping ¼" in center. Tuck ends into wreath and glue to secure.

3. Cut remaining sprig of ivy in half. Glue one piece to the left and one to the right of top center birdhouse. Tuck ends into wreath and glue to secure.

4. Glue one bird to toothpick on birdhouse C. Glue remaining three birds to wreath in ivy at bottom of wreath.

——*Design by Linda Wyszynski*

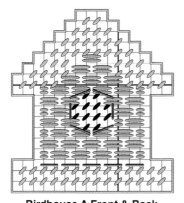

Birdhouse A Front & Back
15 holes x 17 holes
Cut 2, stitch 1

Fig. 1
Horizontal Brick Stitch

Bring needle up at 1,
down at 2, up at 3,
down at 4, etc.

COLOR KEY	
Plastic Canvas Yarn	**Yards**
■ Black #12	2
▨ Tan #334	2
▨ Honey gold #645	3
▨ Seafoam #684	5
▨ Cameo rose #759	4
▨ Blue gray #807	4
▨ Windsor blue #808	2
✎ Seafoam #684 Straight Stitch	
✎ Cameo rose #759 Backstitch	
✎ Blue gray #807 Backstitch	
Color numbers given are for J. & P. Coats Article E.46 plastic canvas yarn.	

Fig. 2
Lazy Kalem Stitch

Bring needle up at 1,
down at 2, up at 3,
down at 4, etc.

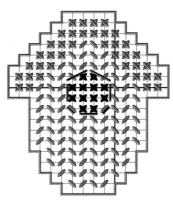

Birdhouse B Front & Back
15 holes x 17 holes
Cut 2, stitch 1

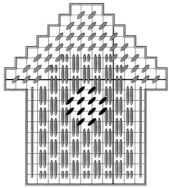

Birdhouse C Front & Back
15 holes x 17 holes
Cut 2, stitch 1

Fig. 3
Vertical Brick Stitch

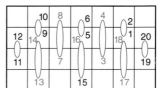

Bring needle up at 1,
down at 2, up at 3,
down at 4, etc.

Santa Fe Baskets

Although they look like they were coiled, these attractive baskets are actually stitched on 7-count plastic canvas! They're perfect for holding potpourri in the bedroom, bath or living room.

Skill Level: Advanced

Project Notes

Use single strand of yarn for Whipstitching and two strands for Long Stitching.

In order to cover cord well and give basket a neat, flat finish, keep yarn smooth and untangled, releasing needle as necessary to allow yarn to unwind.

While Long Stitching, there will be an occasional Crossover Stitch, which is a Long Stitch worked over the present stitching row and the previously stitched row.

Basket A

Materials

- 1 sheet 7-count plastic canvas
- 3" plastic canvas radial circle
- Uniek Needloft plastic canvas yarn as listed in color key
- 20" ⅛" leather lacing
- 7 yards ³⁄₁₆" cotton clothesline cord
- 17mm nickel heart-shaped concho
- 2 (7mm) wooden beads

- 2 (6mm x 9mm) silver pony beads
- White sewing thread
- Craft or hot glue

Instructions

1. Cut plastic canvas according to graphs. Circle will remain uncut and unstitched.

2. Whipstitch basket sides together with sandstone and teal following graphs. Whipstitch basket lip pieces together with teal.

3. To keep clothesline cord from unraveling, wrap cut end tightly with sewing thread; clip thread close to wrapping. Place wrapped end of cord along bottom of basket sides. Following graph, Long Stitch over cord while wrapping cord around basket. Stitch around entire bottom of basket, stitching twice in holes adjacent to side seams as necessary to cover cord.

4. Near end of first row, bring cord up so it lies above first row. Continue Long Stitching over cord around basket for second row of coiled basket, working Crossover Stitches following graph. ***Note:*** *Crossover Stitches may also be used as necessary to cover area when starting a new row of stitching.*

5. Continue wrapping cord around basket and

Long Stitching following graph, stitching seven rows of sandstone, then three rows of teal.

6. With teal, Whipstitch bottom edge of lip sides to top edge of basket sides. Continue wrapping cord around basket and Long Stitching. ***Note:*** *For this row, the top of each stitch will be in the bottom row of holes on lip sides.*

7. For last row, work stitches over cord and top edge of canvas and around backside of lips. When near end of row, cut cord to fit, binding cord end with sewing thread; complete stitching. With sandstone, Whipstitch radial circle to bottom edges of basket sides.

8. Thread ends of leather lacing through concho, crossing lace as though lacing a shoe, leaving a large loop. Slip loop over top of basket and adjust to fit.

9. Thread one silver then one wooden bead on each end of lacing. Glue wooden bead to lacing to hold beads in place.

Basket B

Materials

- 1 sheet 7-count plastic canvas
- 3" plastic canvas radial circle
- Uniek Needloft plastic canvas yarn as listed in color key
- 20" ⅛" leather lacing
- 7 yards ³⁄₁₆" cotton clothesline cord
- 1⅜" x 1¾" gold thunderbird concho
- 2 (8mm) gold cube pony beads
- Large red feather
- Small white feather
- White sewing thread
- Hot-glue gun

Instructions

1. Cut plastic canvas according to graphs. Circle will remain uncut and unstitched.

2. Whipstitch basket sides together with black, red and white following graphs. Whipstitch basket lip pieces together with white.

3. Following steps 3–7 of Basket A, stitch six rows of black, one row of red and five rows of white, Whipstitching lip pieces to basket sides with white before finishing top portion of basket. With black, Whipstitch radial circle to bottom edges of basket sides.

4. Thread ends of leather lacing through concho, crossing lace as though lacing a shoe, leaving a large loop. Slip loop over top of basket and adjust to fit.

5. Thread one bead on each end of lacing. Tie ends in a knot to hold bead in place. Glue feathers together with a small amount of glue. Glue feathers behind concho.

—Designs by Ruby Thacker

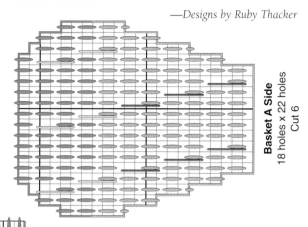

Basket A Side
18 holes x 22 holes
Cut 6

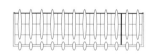

Basket A Lip
12 holes x 3 holes
Cut 6

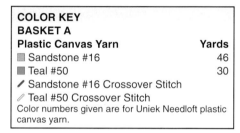

COLOR KEY
BASKET A

Plastic Canvas Yarn	Yards
Sandstone #16	46
Teal #50	30
Sandstone #16 Crossover Stitch	
Teal #50 Crossover Stitch	

Color numbers given are for Uniek Needloft plastic canvas yarn.

Basket B Lip
12 holes x 3 holes
Cut 6

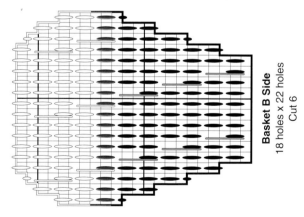

Basket B Side
18 holes x 22 holes
Cut 6

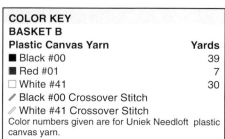

COLOR KEY
BASKET B

Plastic Canvas Yarn	Yards
Black #00	39
Red #01	7
White #41	30
Black #00 Crossover Stitch	
White #41 Crossover Stitch	

Color numbers given are for Uniek Needloft plastic canvas yarn.

Blue Poppies Luncheon Set

Need a pretty table set in a jiffy? Work this vibrant place mat, coaster and napkin ring set by stitching blue and red yarn accents on white plastic canvas. Clever, indeed!

Skill Level: Beginner

Materials
- 1¼ sheets white 7-count Uniek Quick-Count plastic canvas
- Uniek Needloft plastic canvas yarn as listed in color key
- Uniek Needloft Craft Cord as listed in color key
- #16 tapestry needle
- 3¾" square 14-count metallic gold perforated paper by Yarn Tree Designs
- Craft glue

Instructions

1. Cut place mat, coaster, napkin ring and flower from white plastic canvas according to graphs.

2. Following place mat graph with the end on the left and the center on the right, stitch flowers on left border with royal yarn and gold cord. Turn graph so the center is on the left and the end is on the right, then stitch flowers on right border. Complete place mat with Christmas red Backstitches following graph.

3. Stitch flowers on coaster with royal yarn and gold cord following graph, then Backstitch with Christmas red. Backstitch napkin ring with Christmas red, overlapping four holes before stitching. Do not Overcast place mat, coaster and napkin ring.

4. Stitch flower following graph. Overcast petals

Blue Poppies Coaster
25 holes x 25 holes
Cut 1

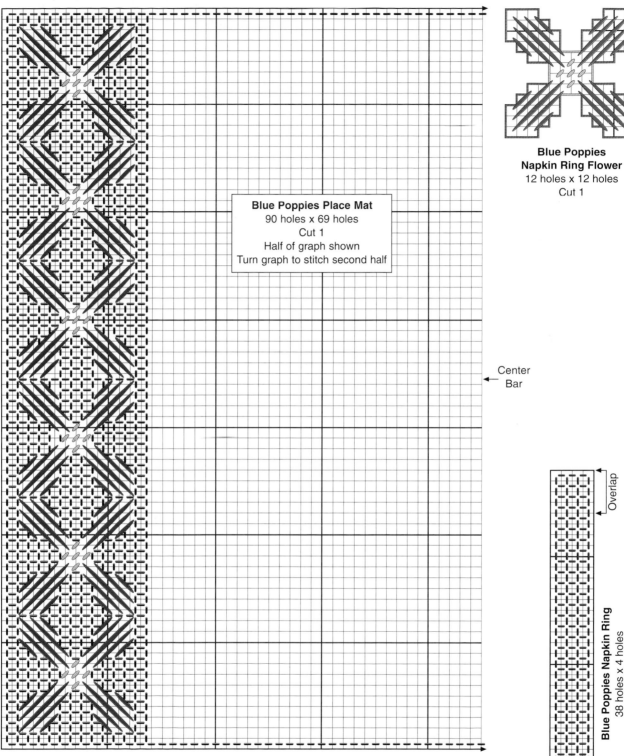

Blue Poppies Place Mat
90 holes x 69 holes
Cut 1
Half of graph shown
Turn graph to stitch second half

← Center Bar

Blue Poppies Napkin Ring Flower
12 holes x 12 holes
Cut 1

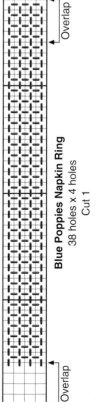

Overlap

Blue Poppies Napkin Ring
38 holes x 4 holes
Cut 1

Overlap

with royal. With gold cord, Whipstitch center of flower to napkin ring at overlap where indicated on flower graph.

5. To line coaster, apply glue to backside of coaster. Place white side of gold perforated paper on glue. Allow to dry.

—*Designs by Mary T. Cosgrove*

COLOR KEY	
Plastic Canvas Yarn	**Yards**
■ Royal #32	16
✁ Christmas red #02 Backstitch	47
Craft Cord	
▨ Gold #01	3
Color numbers given are for Uniek Needloft plastic canvas yarn and craft cord.	

Table Textures

The perfect project for beginning stitchers, this table set includes a place mat and napkin rings.

Skill Level: Beginner

Materials

- 1½ sheets 7-count plastic canvas
- Uniek Needloft plastic canvas yarn as listed in color key
- 8" x 11" piece off-white felt
- Hot-glue gun

Instructions

1. Cut plastic canvas according to graphs.

2. Work pieces with a Rice Stitch following graphs and Fig. 1, working eggshell stitches first. Work one row of burgundy top stitches around place mat for border and on napkin rings. Work center of place mat with navy top stitches.

3. Using burgundy throughout, Overcast place mat and top and bottom edges of napkin rings. Whipstitch short edges of one napkin ring together. Repeat with second napkin ring.

4. Center and glue felt to backside of place mat.

—*Designs by Jeanette Vanetta*

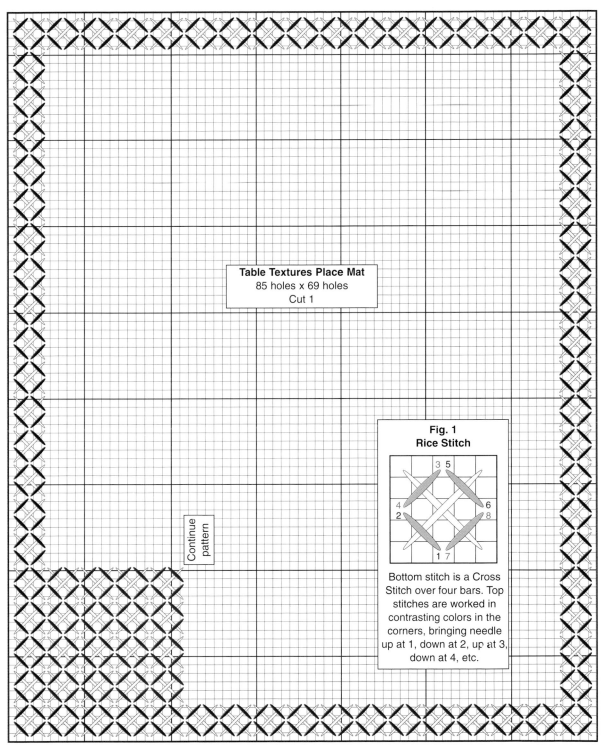

Table Textures Place Mat
85 holes x 69 holes
Cut 1

Continue pattern

**Fig. 1
Rice Stitch**

Bottom stitch is a Cross Stitch over four bars. Top stitches are worked in contrasting colors in the corners, bringing needle up at 1, down at 2, up at 3, down at 4, etc.

COLOR KEY

Plastic Canvas Yarn	Yards
■ Burgundy #03	16
■ Navy #31	30
☐ Eggshell #39	37

Color numbers given are for Uniek Needloft plastic canvas yarn.

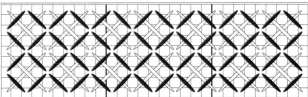

Table Textures Napkin Ring
29 holes x 9 holes
Cut 2

Fruit Recipe Box

Keep all your favorite recipes at your fingertips with this colorful recipe box stitched on 10-count plastic canvas.

Skill Level: Intermediate

Materials

- 2 sheets 10-count plastic canvas
- DMC #3 pearl cotton as listed in color key
- DMC 6-strand embroidery floss as listed in color key

Instructions

1. Cut plastic canvas according to graphs. Cut two 31-hole x 49-hole pieces for box sides, one 31-hole x 68-hole piece for box bottom, two 33-hole x 5-hole pieces for lid short sides and two 70-hole x 5-hole pieces for lid long sides. Box bottom will remain unstitched.

2. Stitch box front, box back and lid top with pearl cotton. Work Backstitches with 3 strands floss when background stitching is completed.

3. Using white pearl cotton through step 5, stitch lid sides and box sides with horizontal Slanting Gobelin Stitches (lower left to upper right) worked over two bars as with box front, back and lid top.

4. Overcast top edges of box front, back and sides and bottom edges of lid sides. Whipstitch box front and back to box sides, then Whipstitch box bottom to box front, back and sides.

5. Whipstitch lid sides together, then Whipstitch lid sides to lid top.

—Design by Phyllis Dobbs

COLOR KEY	
#3 Pearl Cotton	**Skeins**
☐ White	7
▨ Medium lavender #208	1
■ Christmas red #321	1
▨ Medium mahogany #400	1
☐ Very dark Christmas red #489	1
■ Medium violet #552	1
☐ Dark lavender #554	1
■ Light cranberry #603	1
▨ Plum #718	1
☐ Deep canary #725	1
☐ Off-white #746	1
▨ Very dark apricot #900	1
▨ Christmas green #909	1
▨ Nile #913	1
☐ Dark plum #915	1
▨ Pumpkin #971	1
6-Strand Embroidery Floss	
╱ Very dark blue green #500 Backstitch	1
╱ Very dark violet #550 Backstitch	1
╱ Medium topaz #782 Backstitch	1
╱ Very dark garnet #902 Backstitch	1
╱ Copper #919 Backstitch	1
Color numbers given are for DMC #3 pearl cotton and 6-strand embroidery floss.	

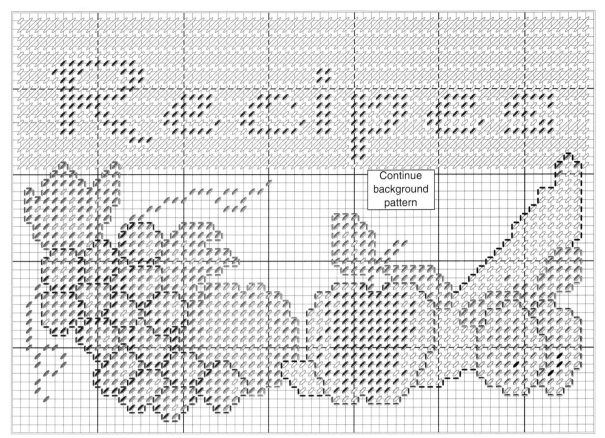

Continue background pattern

Recipe Box Front & Back
68 holes x 49 holes
Cut 2
Stitch front as graphed
Stitch back with white
Slanting Gobelin Stitches only

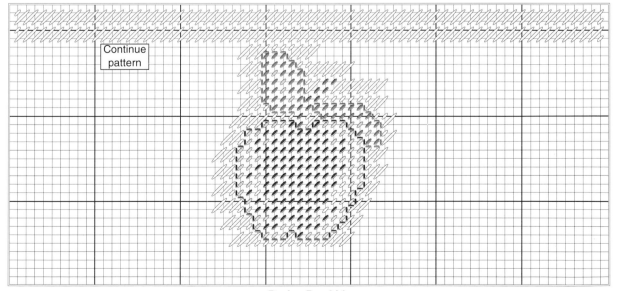

Continue pattern

Recipe Box Lid
70 holes x 33 holes
Cut 1

Pretty Roses Place Mat

Stitch a set of four, six or eight of these lovely place mats. Perfect for any meal or occasion, you'll find yourself using them again and again!

Skill Level: Beginner

Materials
- 12" x 18" sheet Darice Super Soft 7-count plastic canvas
- Uniek Needloft plastic canvas yarn as listed in color key
- #16 tapestry needle

Instructions
1. Using entire sheet of plastic canvas for place mat and following place mat graph with the end on the right and the center on the left, stitch plastic canvas to center.

2. Turn graph so the center is on the right and the end is on the left. Continue stitching from center until mat is completed, making sure not to repeat any stitches already worked on or past the center bar.

3. Overcast edges with eggshell.

—*Design by Angie Arickx*

COLOR KEY	
Plastic Canvas Yarn	**Yards**
■ Lavender #05	13
☐ Eggshell #39	110
■ Camel #43	13
■ Teal #50	16
Color numbers given are for Uniek Needloft plastic canvas yarn.	

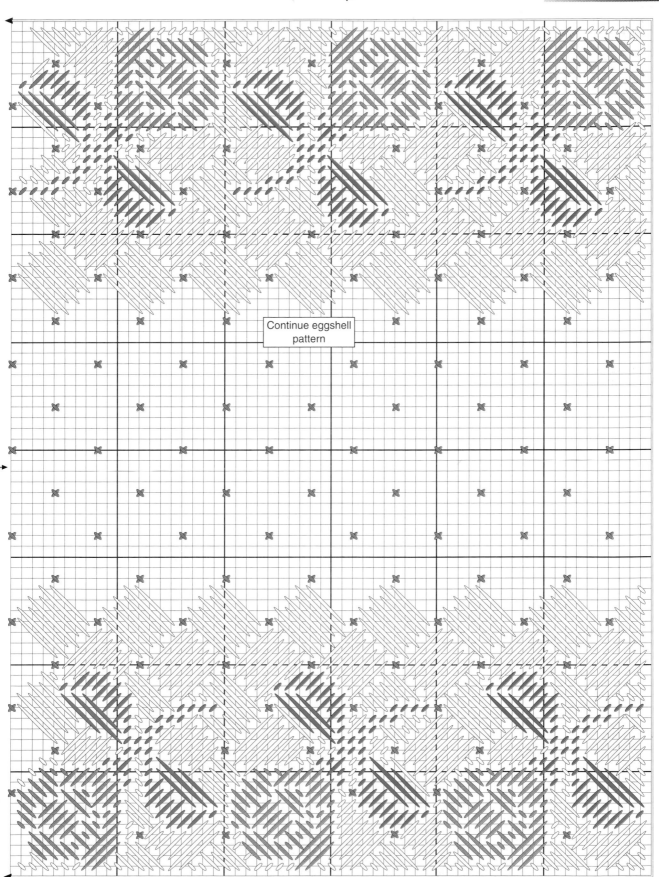

Continue eggshell
pattern

Center
Bar →

Pretty Roses Place Mat
120 holes x 80 holes
Stitch first half as shown
Turn graph and stitch second half

Terrific Tissue Toppers

What's fun, practical, colorful and a great gift idea all in one?
Tissue box covers! An all-time favorite of plastic canvas
stitchers everywhere, tissue toppers make great bazaar crafts,
too. Following is a collection of ten terrific tissue box covers
in a variety of colors, styles and designs.

Pretty Pastels

Dress up your bedroom or bath with this lovely tissue box cover and potpourri holder set. Soft pastels worked in a lovely eight-pointed star create a pretty combination everyone will love!

Skill Level: Beginner

Materials

- 2¼ sheets 7-count plastic canvas
- Spinrite Bernat Berella "4" worsted weight yarn as listed in color key
- #16 tapestry needle
- 3⅝" square off-white felt
- Hot-glue gun

Instructions

1. Cut plastic canvas according to graphs (right and page 66). Cut one 31-hole x 31-hole piece for potpourri holder bottom. Holder bottom will remain unstitched.

2. Stitch pieces with Slanting Gobelin Stitches first, then Continental Stitches following graphs.

3. For tissue box cover, using periwinkle throughout, Overcast inside edges of top and bottom edges of sides. Whipstitch sides together, then sides to top.

4. For potpourri holder, using natural throughout,

Overcast top edges of sides. Whipstitch sides together, then Whipstitch sides to bottom. Glue felt to bottom of holder, trimming as necessary.

—*Designs by Joan Green*

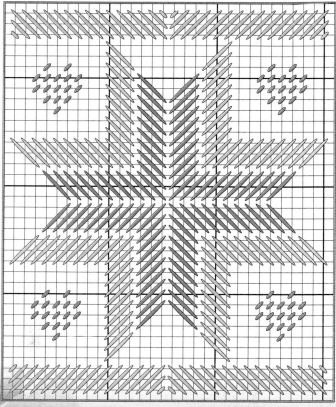

Pretty Pastels Cover Side
31 holes x 37 holes
Cut 4

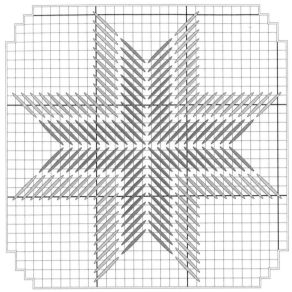

Pretty Pastels Potpourri Holder Side
31 holes x 31 holes
Cut 4

COLOR KEY	
Worsted Weight Yarn	**Yards**
■ Light periwinkle #8803	24
▨ Pale antique rose #8814	15
▨ Pale sea green #8879	28
▨ Rose #8921	16
Uncoded areas are natural	
#8940 Continental Stitches	58
⁄ Natural #8940 Overcasting	
and Whipstitching	
Color numbers given are for Spinrite Bernat Berella "4" worsted weight yarn.	

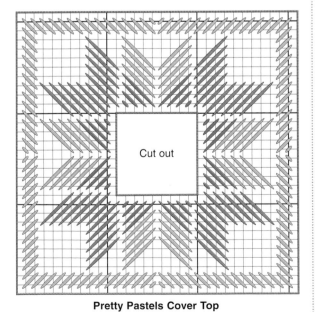

Pretty Pastels Cover Top
31 holes x 31 holes
Cut 1

Spring Bouquet

Every time the winter blues get you down, pull out this colorful project and chase the blues away! Soon you'll have a lovely spring bouquet to lift your spirits all year long!

Skill Level: Beginner

Materials

- 1⅓ sheets 7-count plastic canvas
- J. & P. Coats Plastic Canvas Yarn Art. E.46 as listed in color key
- Anchor 6-strand embroidery floss by Coats & Clark as listed in color key
- 18" ½"-wide light blue satin ribbon
- Sewing needle and light blue sewing thread
- Hot-glue gun (optional)

Instructions

1. Cut plastic canvas according to graphs.

2. Continental Stitch pieces following graphs, stitching uncoded areas with white. Work Backstitches with 6 strands floss over completed background stitching.

3. Using white throughout, Overcast inside edges of top and bottom edges of sides. Whipstitch sides together, then Whipstitch sides to top.

4. Tie ribbon in a bow. Trim ends to a point. With sewing needle and light blue sewing thread, attach bow to cover top where indicated on graph.

Optional: With glue gun, loosely tack ends of ribbon to tissue box sides.

—*Design by Laura Scott*

COLOR KEY	
Plastic Canvas Yarn	**Yards**
☐ Yellow #230	4
▨ Sea coral #246	5
▨ Medium coral #252	5
▨ Light seafoam #683	11
■ Grenadine #730	5
▨ Blue jewel #818	15
Uncoded areas are white	
#1 Continental Stitches	55
⁄ White #1 Overcasting and Whipstitching	
6-Strand Embroidery Floss	**Skeins**
⁄ Dark aquamarine #187 Backstitch and Straight Stitch	1
Color numbers given are for J. & P. Coats Article E.46 plastic canvas yarn and Anchor embroidery floss.	

Spring Bouquet Side
30 holes x 36 holes
Cut 4

Spring Bouquet Top
30 holes x 30 holes
Cut 1

Cut out

Pretty in Pink

Whether for a new baby girl's nursery or for anyone who loves pink, this enchanting tissue box cover is sure to delight her!

Skill Level: Intermediate

Materials

- 1⅓ sheets 7-count plastic canvas
- Plastic canvas yarn (2 oz per skein) as listed in color key
- #16 tapestry needle

Instructions

1. Cut plastic canvas according to graphs.

2. Stitch pieces with pink yarn following graphs. Fill in background with white Continental Stitches.

3. With pink, Overcast bottom edges of sides and inside edges of top. Whipstitch sides together, then Whipstitch sides to top.

4. Cut one 13" length each from pink and white yarn. Thread both lengths under center pink stitch where indicated on graph. Make ends even; tie in a bow.

—*Design by Roseanna Beck*

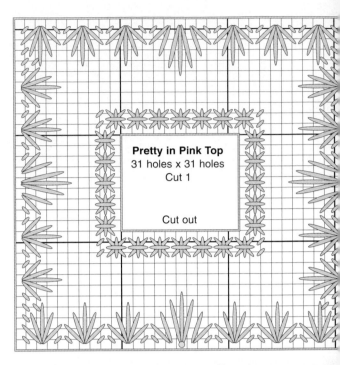

Pretty in Pink Top
31 holes x 31 holes
Cut 1

Cut out

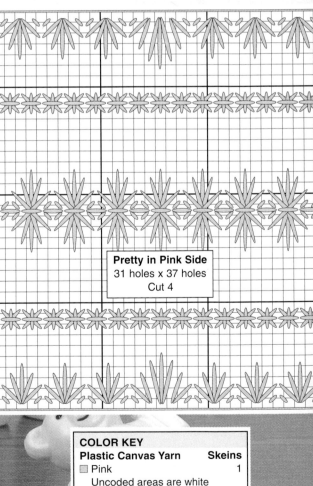

Pretty in Pink Side
31 holes x 37 holes
Cut 4

COLOR KEY

Plastic Canvas Yarn	Skeins
☐ Pink	1
Uncoded areas are white Continental Stitches	1
○ Attach bow	

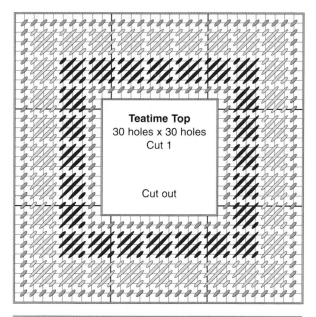

Teatime Top
30 holes x 30 holes
Cut 1

Cut out

Teatime

Invite a friend over for a slice of fresh-baked pie and a cup of tea, and be sure to have this coordinating accent close by for the occasion!

Skill Level: Beginner

Materials

- 1⅓ sheets 7-count plastic canvas
- Uniek Needloft plastic canvas yarn as listed in color key
- DMC #3 pearl cotton as listed in color key

Instructions

1. Cut plastic canvas according to graphs.

2. Continental Stitch pieces following graphs, stitching uncoded areas with white. Work Backstitches and French Knots with 2 strands pearl cotton over completed background stitching.

3. Using cerulean throughout, Overcast inside edges of top and bottom edges of sides. Whipstitch sides together, then Whipstitch sides to top.

—Design by Michele Wilcox

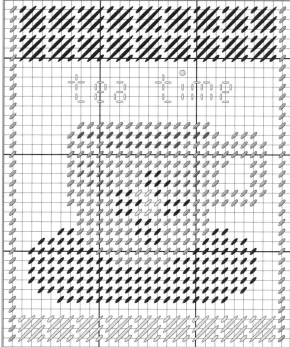

Teatime Side
30 holes x 36 holes
Cut 4

COLOR KEY	
Plastic Canvas Yarn	**Yards**
■ Rose #06	25
▨ Cinnamon #14	3
☐ Straw #19	9
▨ Forest #29	4
▨ Cerulean #34	32
Uncoded areas are white #41 Continental Stitches	24
#3 Pearl Cotton	
⁄ Light antique blue #932 Backstitch	4
○ Light antique blue #932 French Knot	
Color numbers given are for Uniek Needloft plastic canvas yarn and DMC #3 pearl cotton.	

Vanity Organizer and Summer Roses

Here's a great idea for today's busy working woman—a makeup organizer and tissue box cover in one attractive design! Stitch it in classic cream, or another color to suit your decor. Or, stitch a bouquet of beautiful roses as a cherished and romantic gift, perfect for birthdays, anniversaries and Mother's Day.

Vanity Organizer

Skill Level: Advanced

Materials

- 2 sheets 7-count plastic canvas
- Worsted weight yarn as listed in color key

Instructions

1. Cut plastic canvas according to graphs (right and pages 72 and 73).

2. Using cream through step 6, stitch pieces following graphs. Stitch one organizer front as graphed. Second organizer front will remain unstitched. For cover front and organizer bottom only, do not stitch over bar with blue line. Overcast inside edges of cover top and bottom edges of cover sides and cover back.

3. With wrong sides together, Whipstitch top edges of two organizer sides together. Repeat with remaining two organizer sides. With wrong sides together, Whipstitch top edges of organizer divider pieces together.

4. Following Fig. 1 throughout assembly (page 72), Whipstitch bottom edges of divider to organizer bottom where indicated on organizer bottom graph with blue line. Place stitched organizer front on unstitched organizer front and Whipstitch bottom edges to front edge of organizer bottom. Whipstitch

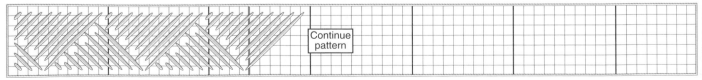

Vanity Organizer Front
68 holes x 7 holes
Cut 2, stitch 1

Continued on next page

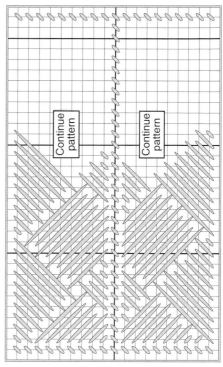

Vanity Cover Side
33 holes x 20 holes
Cut 2

Continue pattern

Continue pattern

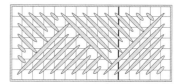

Vanity Organizer Divider
15 holes x 7 holes
Cut 2

divider to unstitched organizer front where indicated on organizer front graph with blue line.

5. Whipstitch organizer sides to organizer front, working through all four pieces of canvas. Whipstitch top edges of organizer front pieces together. Whipstitch organizer sides to organizer bottom.

6. Whipstitch back edge of organizer bottom to bottom edge of cover front. Whipstitch remaining side edges of divider to cover front and where indicated on graph with blue line.

7. Whipstitch cover sides to cover front, working through all four pieces where needed. Whipstitch remaining side edges of cover sides to cover back. Whipstitch cover top to cover front, back and sides.

—*Design by Kristine Loffredo*

Summer Roses

Skill Level: Intermediate

Materials
- 1⅓ sheets 7-count plastic canvas
- Worsted weight yarn as listed in color key

Instructions

1. Cut plastic canvas according to the graphs (page 74).

2. Continental Stitch pieces following graphs. Using burgundy throughout, Overcast inside edges of top and bottom edges of sides. Whipstitch sides together, then Whipstitch sides to top.

—*Design by Conn Baker Gibney*

Fig. 1
Assembly Diagram

Cover Top

Tray Bottom
Tray Side

Cover Front

Tray Divider

Tray Side

Tray Front

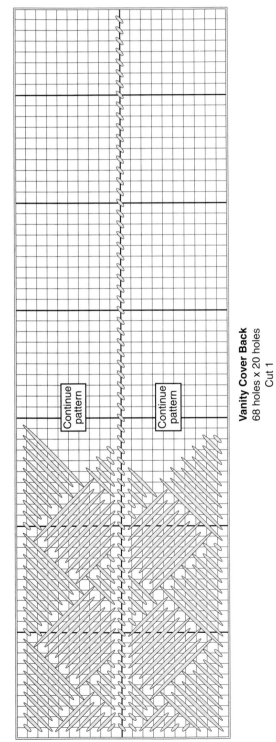

Continue pattern

Continue pattern

Vanity Cover Back
68 holes x 20 holes
Cut 1

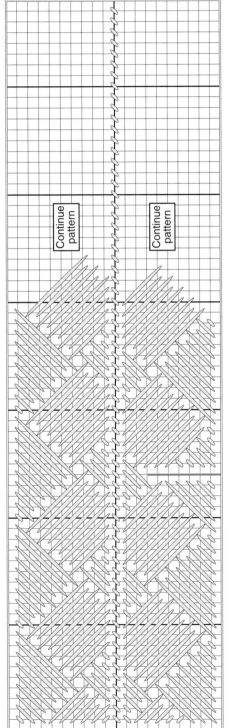

Continue pattern

Continue pattern

Vanity Cover Front
68 holes x 20 holes
Cut 1

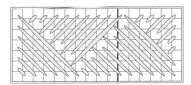

Vanity Organizer Side
16 holes x 7 holes
Cut 4

COLOR KEY

Worsted Weight Yarn	Yards
☐ Cream	100

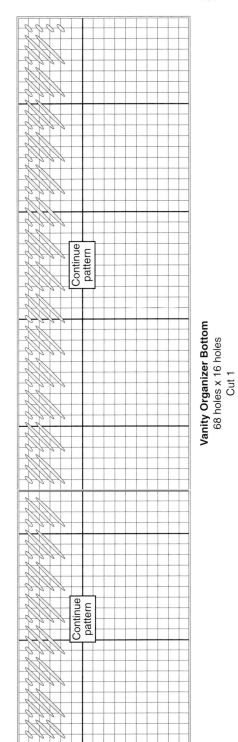

Continue pattern

Continue pattern

Vanity Organizer Bottom
68 holes x 16 holes
Cut 1

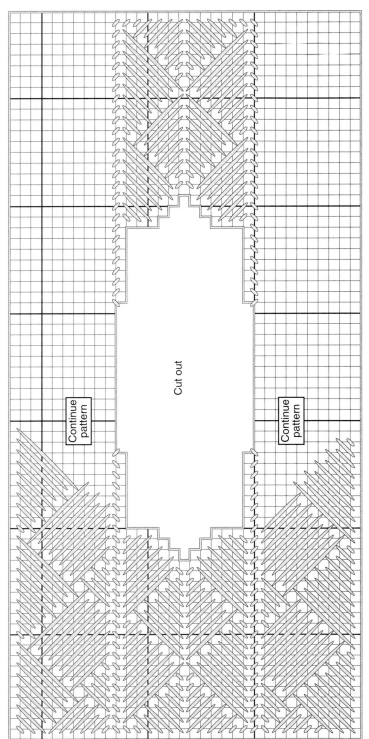

Continue pattern

Continue pattern

Cut out

Vanity Cover Top
68 holes x 33 holes
Cut 1

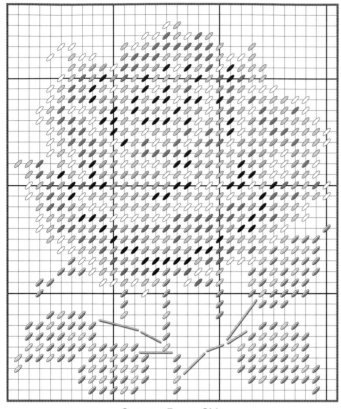

Summer Roses Side
31 holes x 37 holes
Cut 4

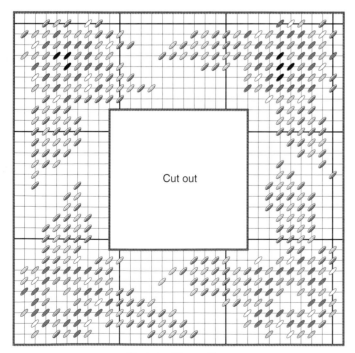

Summer Roses Top
31 holes x 31 holes
Cut 1

COLOR KEY

Worsted Weight Yarn	Yards
▢ Pink	14
◼ Medium rose	14
◼ Medium olive	14
▢ White	10
◨ Cherry pink	9
▢ Light olive	8
◼ Dark rose	6
Uncoded areas are medium orchid Continental Stitches	32
╱ Medium orchid Overcasting and Whipstitching	
╱ Medium olive Backstitch and Straight Stitch	

Tiger Lilies

Capture the beauty of the tiger lily, one of summer's most exotic flowers!

Skill Level: Advanced

Materials

- 1⅓ sheets 7-count plastic canvas
- Worsted weight yarn as listed in color key
- DMC #3 pearl cotton as listed in color key
- DMC #5 pearl cotton as listed in color key

Instructions

1. Cut plastic canvas according to graphs.

2. Continental Stitch pieces following graphs. Work embroidery when Continental Stitching is completed.

3. Overcast inside edges of top with black. Using medium denim throughout, Overcast bottom edges of sides. Whipstitch sides together, alternating sides A and B; Whipstitch sides to top.

— Design by Conn Baker Gibney

COLOR KEY

Worsted Weight Yarn	Yards
▢ White	15
◼ Light sea green	11
◨ Denim blue	10
◨ Dark peach	10
◼ Burnt orange	3
◼ Medium orchid	2
▢ Yellow	2
Uncoded areas are black Continental Stitches	50
╱ Black Backstitch and Overcasting	
╱ Light sea green Straight Stitch	
╱ Burnt orange Straight Stitch	
╱ Medium orchid Straight Stitch	
● Light sea green French Knot	
#3 Pearl Cotton	
╱ Ultra light avocado green #472 Backstitch	3
#5 Pearl Cotton	
● Black #310 French Knot	4
● Dark plum #915 French Knot	4
Color numbers given are for DMC #3 and #5 pearl cotton.	

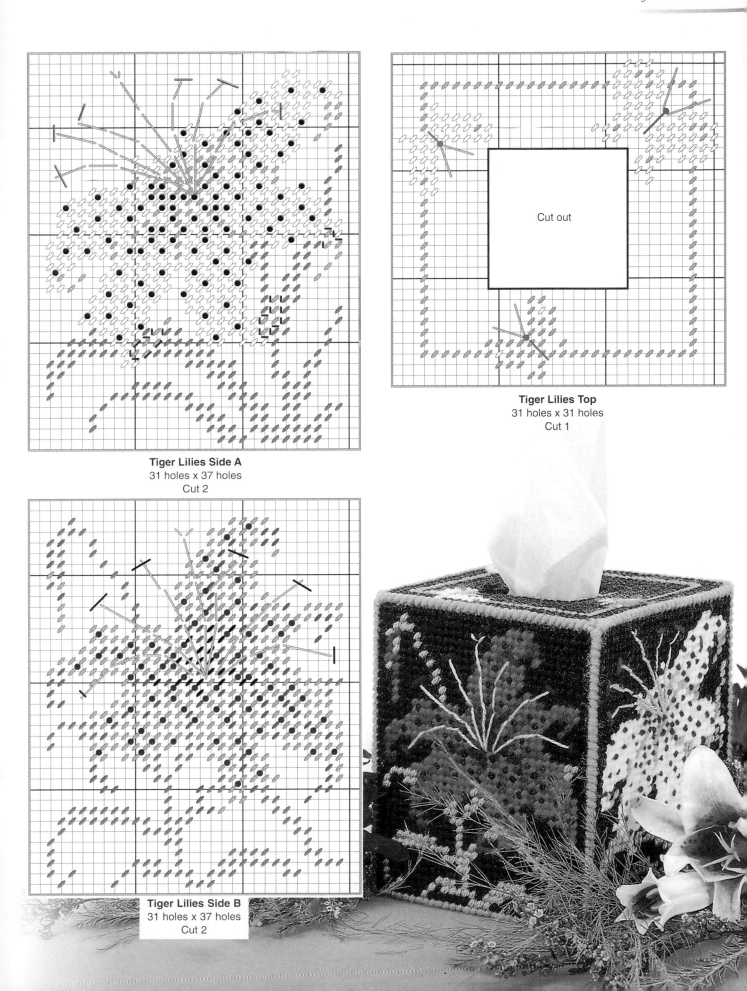

Tiger Lilies Side A
31 holes x 37 holes
Cut 2

Tiger Lilies Top
31 holes x 31 holes
Cut 1

Cut out

Tiger Lilies Side B
31 holes x 37 holes
Cut 2

Snuggly Bears

Youngsters will adore this sweet and decorative tissue box cover with Mama bear securely holding her little Baby bear.

Skill Level: Beginner

Materials

- 2 sheets 7-count plastic canvas
- Uniek Needloft plastic canvas yarn as listed in color key
- DMC #3 pearl cotton as listed in color key
- 8" ¼"-wide red satin ribbon
- Glue gun

Instructions

1. Cut plastic canvas according to graphs (page 77).

2. Stitch pieces following graphs, reversing one arm and one foot before stitching. Work embroidery when background stitching is completed.

3. Overcast all bear pieces following graphs. For tissue box cover, using baby blue throughout, Overcast inside edges of top and bottom edges of sides. Whipstitch sides together, then Whipstitch sides to top.

4. Using photo as a guide through step 5, center and glue large teddy bear to one cover side, making sure bottom edges are even. Glue large teddy bear legs to lower body.

5. Tie red ribbon in a bow around small teddy bear's neck, trimming ends as desired. Glue large teddy arms at shoulders, place small teddy behind arms on body front and glue to secure.

—*Design by Michele Wilcox*

COLOR KEY	
Plastic Canvas Yarn	**Yards**
■ Cinnamon #14	4
□ Lemon #20	5
■ Denim #33	25
▨ Cerulean #34	24
□ Beige #40	4
▨ Camel #43	18
▨ Flesh tone #56	1
Uncoded areas are baby blue #36 Continental Stitches	40
╱ Baby blue #36 Overcasting and Whipstitching	
#3 Pearl Cotton	
╱ Black #310 Backstitch	1
● Black #310 French Knot	
Color numbers given are for Uniek Needloft plastic canvas yarn and DMC #3 pearl cotton.	

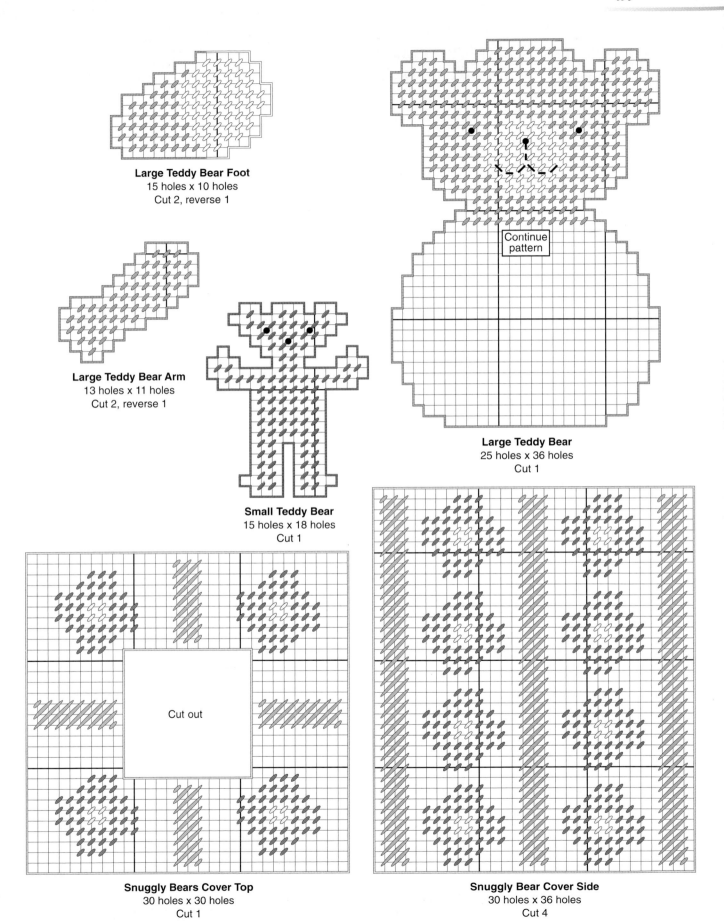

Large Teddy Bear Foot
15 holes x 10 holes
Cut 2, reverse 1

Large Teddy Bear Arm
13 holes x 11 holes
Cut 2, reverse 1

Small Teddy Bear
15 holes x 18 holes
Cut 1

Continue pattern

Large Teddy Bear
25 holes x 36 holes
Cut 1

Cut out

Snuggly Bears Cover Top
30 holes x 30 holes
Cut 1

Snuggly Bear Cover Side
30 holes x 36 holes
Cut 4

Trellis of Roses

Blooming roses and rosebuds adorn a pretty white lattice on this cheerful tissue topper.

Skill Level: Beginner

Materials

- 1⅓ sheets 7-count plastic canvas
- Uniek Needloft plastic canvas yarn as listed in color key

Instructions

1. Cut plastic canvas according to graphs.

2. Continental Stitch pieces following graphs, stitching uncoded areas with denim.

3. Overcast inside edges of top with white. Using mermaid throughout, Overcast bottom edges of sides. Whipstitch sides together, then Whipstitch sides to top.

—Design by Michele Wilcox

COLOR KEY	
Plastic Canvas Yarn	**Yards**
■ Lavender #05	4
▨ Pink #07	7
☐ White #41	24
■ Crimson #42	2
▨ Mermaid #53	12
Uncoded areas are denim	
#33 Continental Stitches	24
Color numbers given are for Uniek Needloft plastic canvas yarn.	

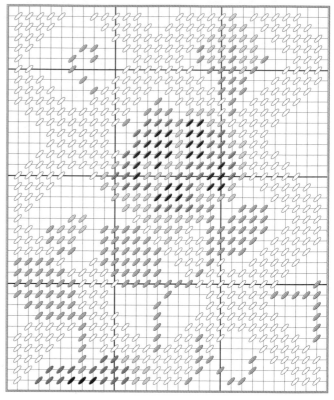

Trellis of Roses Side
30 holes x 36 holes
Cut 4

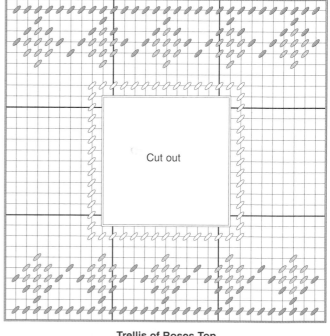

Cut out

Trellis of Roses Top
30 holes x 30 holes
Cut 1

Eight-Pointed Star

Give your home a sampling of country charm
with this pretty quilt star tissue box cover.

Skill Level: Beginner

Materials

- 2 sheets 7-count plastic canvas
- Uniek Needloft plastic canvas yarn as listed in color key
- #16 tapestry needle

Instructions

1. Cut and stitch plastic canvas according to graphs.

2. Using eggshell throughout, Overcast bottom edges of sides and inside edges of top with eggshell. Whipstitch sides together, then Whipstitch sides to top.

—Design by Angie Arickx

COLOR KEY	
Plastic Canvas Yarn	**Yards**
Lavender #05	19
Cerulean #34	24
Eggshell #39	47
Color numbers given are for Uniek Needloft plastic canvas yarn.	

Eight-Pointed Star Side
31 holes x 37 holes
Cut 4

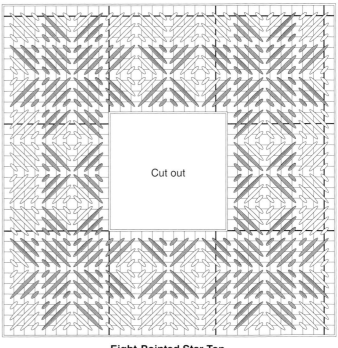

Cut out

Eight-Pointed Star Top
31 holes x 31 holes
Cut 1

Gifts Galore

Whatever the occasion, whether it be a child's birthday, Mother's Day or Father's Day, a bridal or baby shower, or just because, you can stitch the perfect plastic canvas gift in a jiffy! And, because your gift is handcrafted with love, it will be all the more special!

Mountain Forest Set

Do you often find yourself at a loss as to what to give that special man in your life? This handsome three-piece set, including a boutique tissue box cover, trinket box and envelope opener handle, is a perfect masculine gift.

Skill Level: Beginner

Materials

- 2 sheets 7-count plastic canvas
- Darice Nylon Plus plastic canvas yarn as listed in color key
- Metal letter opener with ⅝" x 3" handle
- Tacky craft glue

Instructions

1. Cut plastic canvas according to graphs (page 82). Cut four 22-hole x 12-hole pieces for trinket box sides and one 22-hole x 22-hole piece for trinket box bottom.

2. Stitch pieces following graphs. Continental Stitch trinket box sides and bottom with forest green.

3. Overcast inside edges of tissue box cover top with baby yellow. Using forest green through step 5, Overcast bottom edges of tissue box cover sides. Whipstitch sides together, then Whipstitch sides to top.

4. Overcast top edges of trinket box sides and bottom edges of lid sides. Whipstitch box sides together, then Whipstitch box sides to box bottom. Whipstitch lid sides together, then Whipstitch lid sides to lid top.

5. Overcast bottom edges of letter opener handle. With wrong sides together, Whipstitch handle pieces together along one long side and top. Apply glue to handle of metal letter opener and insert into stitched handle. Whipstitch remaining edges together.

—Designs by Nancy Marshall

COLOR KEY

Plastic Canvas Yarn	Yards
■ Sail blue #04	21
■ Forest green #32	49
■ Camel #34	41
□ Baby yellow #42	7

Uncoded areas are sail blue
#04 Continental Stitches
Color numbers given are for Darice Nylon
Plus plastic canvas yarn.

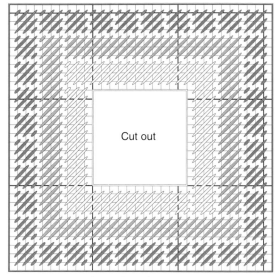

Tissue Box Cover Top
31 holes x 31 holes
Cut 1

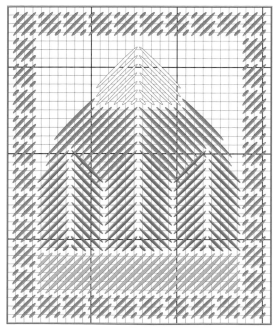

Tissue Box Cover Side
31 holes x 37 holes
Cut 4

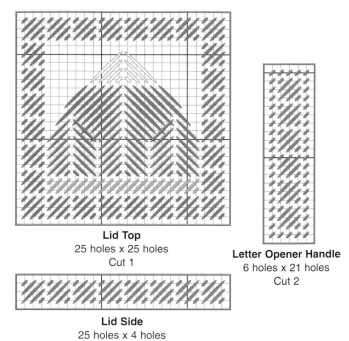

Lid Top
25 holes x 25 holes
Cut 1

Lid Side
25 holes x 4 holes
Cut 4

Letter Opener Handle
6 holes x 21 holes
Cut 2

Shades of Lavender

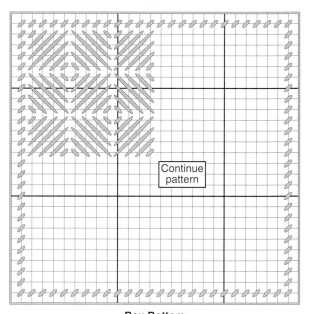

Continue pattern

Box Bottom
27 holes x 27 holes
Cut 1

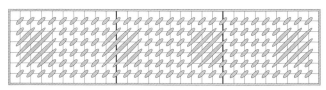

Lid Side
29 holes x 7 holes
Cut 4

Shades of Lavender Gift Box

Beautiful variegated thread, blended with lovely shades of lavender and blue, gives this pretty box an elegant look without extra effort!

Skill Level: Beginner

Materials

- 1 sheet 10-count plastic canvas
- Multi's™ Embellishment cotton/rayon yarn by Bond America as listed in color key
- Kreinik Medium (#16) Braid as listed in color key
- #18 tapestry needle

COLOR KEY	
Cotton/Rayon Yarn	**Spools**
▨ Jeans 'n More #07	3
Medium (#16) Braid	
▨ Amethyst #026	2
Color numbers given are for Multi's Embellishment Yarn by Bond America and Kreinik Medium (#16) Braid.	

- 1¼" yards felt or synthetic suede
- Fabric glue

Project Notes

Be careful when cutting plastic canvas. It is easy to snip through the canvas to be used. If this should happen, stitch as though the hole is still intact and later secure the stitch with a dab of fabric glue.

Be careful not to pull the yarn too tightly.

Instructions

1. Cut plastic canvas according to graphs (pages 82 and 83).

2. For lining, cut four pieces felt or synthetic suede to fit box sides, one piece to fit box bottom, four pieces to fit lid sides and one piece to fit lid top.

3. Stitch pieces with doubled yarn and medium braid following graphs. Using three strands of medium braid, Straight Stitch amethyst star on lid top over completed background stitching.

4. Using yarn throughout, Whipstitch box sides together, then Whipstitch sides to box bottom. Whipstitch lid sides together, then Whipstitch sides to lid top. Overcast top edges of box sides and bottom edges of lid sides.

5. Glue lining inside box and lid, trimming as necessary to fit.

—Design by Bond America

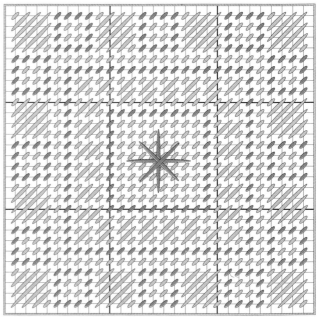

Lid Top
29 holes x 29 holes
Cut 1

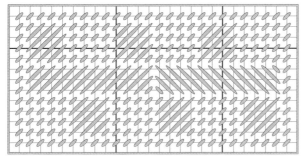

Box Side
27 holes x 14 holes
Cut 4

Jewelry Accents

Fun moon and star buttons make a pair of striking Man in the Moon Earrings! Our attractive Morning Dew set includes a pin and earrings.

Man in the Moon Earrings

Skill Level: Beginner

Materials

- Small amount 14-count plastic canvas
- DMC 6-strand embroidery floss as listed in color key
- Kreinik Medium (#16) Braid as listed in color key
- Kreinik ¹⁄₁₆" Ribbon as listed in color key
- 2 Man in the Moon ceramic buttons #86129 from Mill Hill Products by Gay Bowles Sales, Inc.
- 2 Rosaline Glass Treasures domed matte star charms #12046 from Mill Hill Products by Gay Bowles Sales, Inc.
- Sewing needle and light pink and blue sewing thread
- Pair earring backs
- Black synthetic suede or felt
- Scissors (optional)
- Tacky glue

Instructions

1. Cut plastic canvas according to graphs. Cut two pieces of synthetic suede to fit earrings.

2. Stitch pieces with braid and 6 strands floss following graphs. Overcast edges with ¹⁄₁₆" ribbon, keeping ribbon angled and flat and stitching three times around corners for best coverage.

3. With sewing needle and light pink thread, sew one star to each earring where indicated on graph. With blue thread, sew one ceramic button to center of each earring.

4. For pierced earring, make a hole with scissors in each square of suede or felt approximately ⁵⁄₈" from top corner. Poke earring through hole and glue both post and fabric in place at the same time, trimming edges of backing as necessary. Allow to dry.

5. For clip back, glue suede or felt to backside, trimming edges as necessary. Glue earring back to backside. Allow to dry thoroughly.

—Design by Judi Kauffman

Morning Dew

Skill Level: Beginner

Materials

- ¼ sheet 10-count plastic canvas
- Crystal Rays tubular nylon netting with metallic core by Rainbow Gallery as listed in color key
- Kreinik Medium (#16) Braid as listed in color key
- 1½" pin back
- 4 medium jump rings
- 2 French ear wires
- #22 tapestry needle

Instructions

1. Cut plastic canvas according to graphs.

2. Stitch pieces following graphs. Work Backstitches on pin front when background stitching is completed.

3. Whipstitch wrong sides of two earring pieces together with confetti using two stitches per hole. On the fourth corner, add an extra loop for attaching jump ring. Repeat with remaining two earring pieces.

4. Attach jump ring to extra loop on corner of one earring. Attach a second jump ring and then a French ear wire. Repeat for second earring.

5. Center 1½" pin back on stitched pin back from corner to corner, not side to side; attach with morning dew tubular netting with metallic core.

6. Whipstitch wrong sides of pin front and pin back together with confetti using two stitches per hole.

—Designs by Pat Trumbull

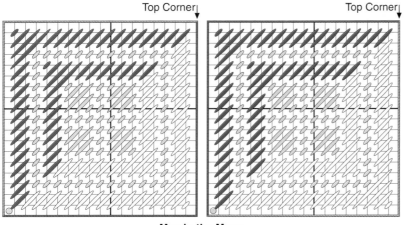

Top Corner | Top Corner

Man in the Moon
18 holes x 18 holes
Cut 1 each

COLOR KEY
MAN IN THE MOON EARRINGS

6-Strand Embroidery Floss	Yards
☐ Very dark royal plum #820	1
☐ Very light antique violet #3743	1
Medium (#16) Braid	
☐ Pearl #032	3
■ Royal #033	3
¹⁄₁₆ " Ribbon	
╱ Royal #033 Overcasting	1
╱ Passion plum #1223 Overcasting	1
○ Attach star	

Color numbers given are for DMC 6-strand embroidery floss and Kreinik Medium (#16) Braid and ¹⁄₁₆ " Ribbon.

COLOR KEY
MORNING DEW

Tubular Netting With Metallic Core	Cards
☐ Morning dew #L119	2
Medium (#16) Braid	**Spools**
╱ Confetti #034 Backstitch and Overcasting	1

Color numbers given are for Crystal Rays tubular nylon netting with metallic core by Rainbow Gallery and Kreinik Medium (#16) Braid.

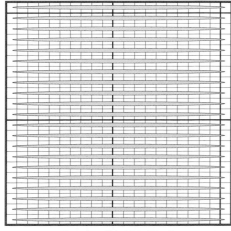

Morning Dew Pin Back
21 holes x 21 holes
Cut 1

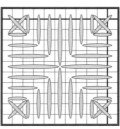

Morning Dew Earring
11 holes x 11 holes
Cut 4

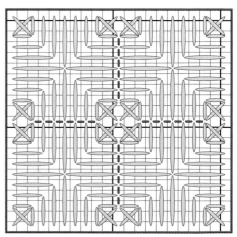

Morning Dew Pin Front
21 holes x 21 holes
Cut 1

Ponytail Decoration

Colorful seed beads stitched onto a small flower-shaped piece of canvas and delicate floral ribbon create a lovely accessory perfect for wearing around a ponytail.

Skill Level: Intermediate

Materials

- Small amount ivory 14-count plastic canvas
- Kreinik ¹⁄₁₆" Ribbon as listed in color key
- Frosted glass seed beads from Mill Hill Products by Gay Bowles Sales, Inc., as listed in color key
- #24 tapestry needle
- #10 crewel needle
- Quilting thread
- 5mm round cabochon by The Beadery: emerald #007
- Narrow braid trim (sample used peach and aquamarine)
- Ivory ponytail accessory
- Craft adhesive

Project Notes

To work beaded areas, use quilting thread and crewel needle. Pour a few beads into a shallow rimmed container. Bring needle up at lower left of first stitch. Pick up bead with needle tip and attach bead with a Half Cross Stitch (from lower left to upper right).

Work horizontal rows from left to right and from right to left with Half Cross Stitches slanting in the same direction. If any beads appear to be loose, stitch through them a second time.

When working with ribbon, keep it smooth and flat. Drop needle occasionally to let ribbon unwind.

Instructions

1. Cut plastic canvas according to graph, rounding off sharp corners.

2. Following project notes and graph, attach beads, weaving thread ends securely through stitching on backside. Using tapestry needle, Overcast edges with ribbon.

3. Glue cabochon to unstitched center of piece; press down for 30 seconds. Allow to dry thoroughly.

4. Using photo as a guide throughout, center and glue stitched piece to ponytail accessory. Glue braid around edge of accessory. Allow to dry.

—Design by Carol Krob

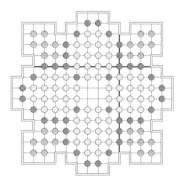

Ponytail Decoration
15 holes x 15 holes
Cut 1

COLOR KEY	
Glass Seed Beads	**Packages**
○ Frosted apricot #62036	1
◐ Frosted aquamarine #62038	1
● Frosted pink coral #62040	1
¹⁄₁₆ " Ribbon	**Yards**
⁄ Star green #9194 Overcasting	2
Color numbers given are for Mill Hill frosted glass seed beads and Kreinik ¹⁄₁₆ " Ribbon.	

Bookworm's (Second) Best Friend

Aside from books, bookmarks are surely an avid reader's best friend! Following is a collection of five very attractive projects sure to be right at home among your best literature.

Golden Quartet

Skill Level: Intermediate

Materials

- ½ sheet black 14-count plastic canvas
- Kreinik Medium (#16) Braid as listed in olor key
- 4 (1"-wide) 10½" lengths black-and-gold ribbon by Bader Trimming Co., Inc.
- Black synthetic suede or felt
- Seam sealant
- Tacky glue

Project Note

Solid black or gold grosgrain, satin or velvet ribbon may be substituted for the black-and-gold ribbon.

Instructions

1. Cut plastic canvas according to graphs (page 88). Cut synthetic suede or felt square to fit each piece.

2. Stitch pieces following graphs and Fig. 1. Do not Overcast pieces.

3. Center and glue ribbon to backside of each stitched square. Glue suede or felt to back of each piece.

4. Apply seam sealant to end of each ribbon. Allow to dry. Cut a clean edge on each ribbon.

—Designs by Judi Kauffman

I Love Books

Skill Level: Beginner

Materials

- ⅛ sheet 14-count plastic canvas
- Anchor 6-strand embroidery floss by Coats & Clark as listed in color key
- Kreinik Medium (#16) Braid as listed in color key
- Kreinik ¹⁄₁₆" Ribbon as listed in color key
- Navy synthetic suede
- Tacky glue

Instructions

1. Cut plastic canvas according to graph (page 88). Cut synthetic suede to fit bookmark.

2. Continental Stitch piece with braid and 6 strands floss following graph. Overcast edges with ¹⁄₁₆" ribbon, keeping ribbon angled and flat and stitching three times around corners for best coverage.

3. Glue synthetic suede to backside of stitched piece, trimming edges as necessary. Allow to dry.

—Design by Judi Kauffman

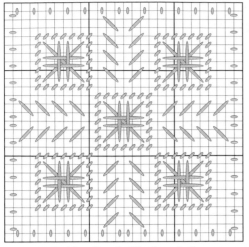

Golden Quartet Bookmark A
28 holes x 28 holes
Cut 1

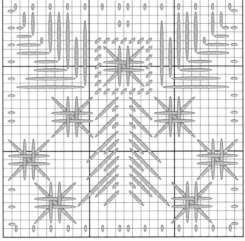

Golden Quartet Bookmark B
28 holes x 28 holes
Cut 1

Golden Quartet Bookmark C
28 holes x 28 holes
Cut 1

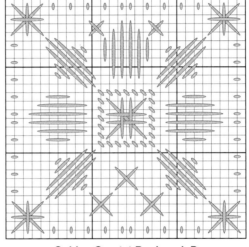

Golden Quartet Bookmark D
28 holes x 28 holes
Cut 1

COLOR KEY	
GOLDEN QUARTET	
Medium (#16) Braid	**Spools**
▨ Aztec gold #202HL	4
Color numbers given are for Kreinik Medium (#16) Braid.	

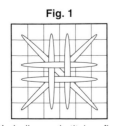

Fig. 1

Work diagonal stitches first,
then stitch vertical and horizontal stitches,
weaving the pattern shown.

COLOR KEY	
I L♥VE B♥♥KS	
6-Strand Embroidery Floss	**Yards**
▨ Bright Christmas red #46	3
▪ Very dark royal blue #134	2
▨ Nile #204	3
▪ Dark drab brown #898	6
Uncoded areas are light beige #390 Continental Stitches	8¾
Medium (#16) Braid	
▪ Red #003HL	3
¹⁄₁₆ " Ribbon	
╱ Royal #033 Overcasting	4
Color numbers given are for Anchor 6-strand embroidery floss and Kreinik Medium (#16) Braid and ¹⁄₁₆ " Ribbon.	

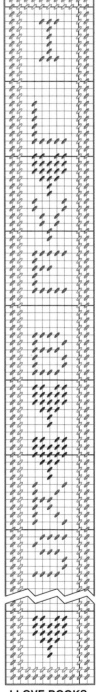

I LOVE BOOKS
12 holes x 122 holes
Cut 1

Argyle Accessories

Here's a gift sure to please that man or woman who has everything. An attractive eyeglasses case with matching business card case will make an appreciated gift!

Skill Level: Intermediate

Materials

- 1½ sheets ecru 14-count plastic canvas
- DMC #3 pearl cotton as listed in color key
- DMC #5 pearl cotton as listed in color key
- 7" square beige brown felt
- Toothpick
- Fabric glue

Eyeglasses Case

1. Cut plastic canvas according to graph (page 90).

2. Stitch piece with #5 pearl cotton following graph. Beginning in upper left-hand corner, work all peach flesh Backstitches, then beginning in the same corner, work all light beige brown Backstitches.

3. Following Fig. 1, work diamond areas with Star Stitches, then fill in around each Star Stitch following Fig. 2.

4. Apply a small amount of glue to edges of felt with toothpick. Glue felt to wrong side of stitched eyeglasses case. Place heavy book on needlework until glue is dry.

5. With wrong sides together, fold case in half. Using light blue #3 pearl cotton throughout, Whipstitch long sides and bottom edges together. Overcast top edge, catching top edge of felt while Overcasting.

Business Card Case

1. Cut card case front and back according to graphs (page 90).

2. Stitch case front following steps 2 and 3 of Eyeglasses Case.

3. Stitch back piece with #5 pearl cotton following graph, keeping the top three rows as neat as possible on the backside. ***Note:*** *Top rows on the backside will be seen from the front.*

4. Using light blue #3 pearl cotton throughout, Overcast top edges of front and back. With wrong sides together, Whipstitch side and bottom edges together.

—*Designs by Linda Wyszynski*

Fig. 1

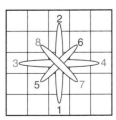

Bring needle up at 1, down at 2, up at 3, down at 4, etc.

Fig. 2

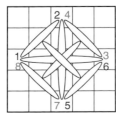

Bring needle up at 1, down at 2, up at 3, down at 4, etc.

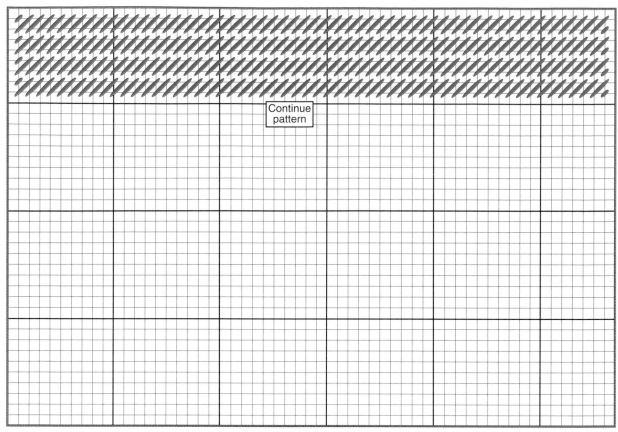

Card Holder Back
57 holes x 39 holes
Cut 1

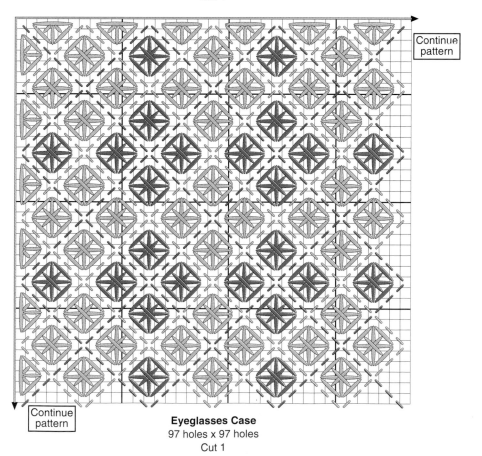

Eyeglasses Case
97 holes x 97 holes
Cut 1

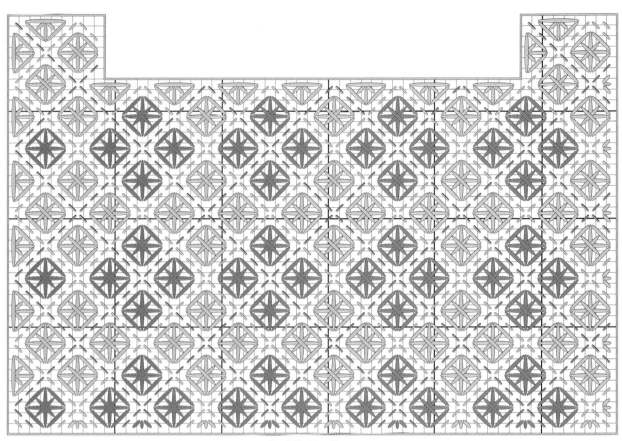

Card Holder Front
57 holes x 39 holes
Cut 1

COLOR KEY	
#3 Pearl Cotton	**Skeins**
⁄ Light blue #826 Overcasting	
and Whipstitching	1
#5 Pearl Cotton	
■ Light blue #826	3
▢ Light beige brown #841	4
⁄ Peach flesh #352 Backstitch	2
⁄ Light beige brown	
#841 Backstitch	
Color numbers given are for DMC #3 and #5 pearl cotton.	

Mini Jewel Boxes

These pretty gift boxes, stitched on 14-count plastic canvas shapes, are just the right size for holding jewelry. Use them on your dresser, or for enclosing a special gift.

Skill Level: Intermediate

Materials

Each Box

- ⅛ sheet 14-count plastic canvas
- RibbonFloss from Rhode Island Textile Co. as listed in color key
- Glass seed beads from Mill Hill Products by Gay Bowles Sales, Inc., as listed in color key
- #24 tapestry needle
- #10 crewel needle
- Quilting thread
- Craft adhesive

Round Box

- 2 (14-count) plastic canvas circles by Darice
- 4 (18mm x 13mm) pear cabochons by The Beadery: frosted pink #015M

Oval Box

- 2 (14-count) plastic canvas ovals by Darice
- 25mm x 18mm oval cabochon by The Beadery: frosted emerald #007M

Heart Box

- 2 (14-count) plastic canvas hearts by Darice
- 15.5mm x 15mm heart cabochon by The Beadery: frosted amethyst #002M

Hexagon Box

- 2 (14-count) plastic canvas hexagons by Darice
- 18mm round cabochon by The Beadery: frosted topaz #023M

Project Notes

To work beaded areas, use quilting thread and crewel needle. Pour a few beads into a shallow rimmed container. Bring needle up at lower left of first stitch. Pick up bead with needle tip and attach bead with a Half Cross Stitch (from lower left to upper right).

Work horizontal rows from left to right and from right to left with Half Cross Stitches slanting in the same direction. Work vertical and diagonal rows from top to bottom. If any beads appear to be

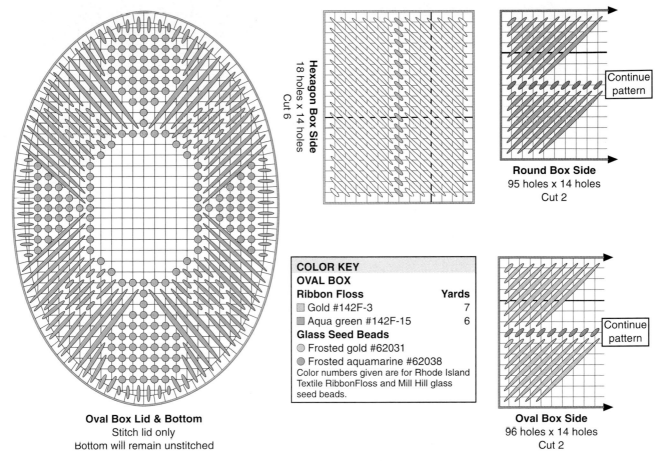

Hexagon Box Side
18 holes x 14 holes
Cut 6

Round Box Side
95 holes x 14 holes
Cut 2

Continue pattern

COLOR KEY
OVAL BOX

Ribbon Floss	Yards
☐ Gold #142F-3	7
☐ Aqua green #142F-15	6

Glass Seed Beads
○ Frosted gold #62031
● Frosted aquamarine #62038
Color numbers given are for Rhode Island Textile RibbonFloss and Mill Hill glass seed beads.

Continue pattern

Oval Box Side
96 holes x 14 holes
Cut 2

Oval Box Lid & Bottom
Stitch lid only
Bottom will remain unstitched

loose, stitch through them a second time. To straighten a long row of beads, run needle back through entire row after completing it.

When working with ribbon floss, keep floss smooth and flat. To prevent twisting and tangling, guide floss between thumb and forefinger of free hand. Drop needle occasionally to let floss unwind.

Instructions

1. Cut box sides from plastic canvas according to graphs (above and page 94).

2. Following project notes and graphs, stitch beaded areas on box lids. Using tapestry needle, stitch remainder of design with ribbon floss, filling in with extra stitches as necessary to cover canvas. Stitch box sides following graphs. Box bottoms will remain unstitched.

3. For round box, using smokey blue throughout, Overcast lid and top edge of side. Whipstitch short ends of side together, then Whipstitch bottom edge of side to box bottom.

4. Glue frosted pink cabochons to unstitched areas on lid. Allow to dry thoroughly. To form a hinge, with smokey blue, tack lid to top edge of box at

seam area with three or four closely spaced stitches.

5. Using aqua green ribbon floss for Overcasting and Whipstitching, finish oval box following steps 3 and 4, centering seam of box side on one long edge of box bottom and box lid. Glue frosted emerald cabochon to unstitched area lid top.

6. For heart box, using purple throughout, Overcast lid and top edges of sides. With right sides together, Whipstitch one short end of sides together. Bring sides down and around; with wrong sides together, Whipstitch remaining short ends together. Whipstitch box bottom to sides.

7. Glue frosted amethyst heart to unstitched area on lid. Allow to dry thoroughly. With purple, tack lid to top edge of box at top center point and at top of each curve at top of heart.

8. For hexagon box, using mist green through step 9, Overcast five lid sides and top edges of five box sides. Whipstitch sides together, then Whipstitch sides to bottom.

9. Glue frosted topaz cabochon to unstitched area on lid. Allow to dry thoroughly. Whipstitch unstitched side of lid to unstitched top edge of side.

—Designs by Carol Krob

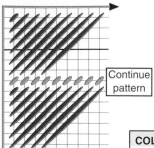

Heart Box Side
46 holes x 14 holes
Cut 2

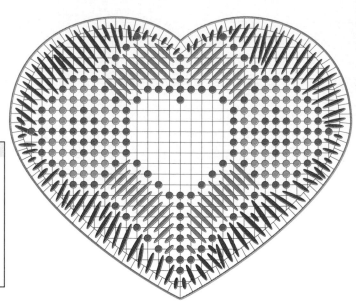

Heart Box Lid & Bottom
Stitch lid only
Bottom will remain unstitched

COLOR KEY
HEART BOX

Ribbon Floss	Yards
Purple #142F-8	5
Black orchid #142F-26	7

Glass Seed Beads
- Frosted mauve #62037
- Frosted royal purple #62042

Color numbers given are for Rhode Island Textile RibbonFloss and Mill Hill seed beads.

Hexagon Box Lid & Bottom
Stitch lid only
Bottom will remain unstitched

COLOR KEY
HEXAGON BOX

Ribbon Floss	Yards
Ecru #142F-4	12
Mist green #142F-20	5½

Glass Seed Beads
- Frosted bottle green #65270
- Frosted apricot #62040

Color numbers given are for Rhode Island Textile RibbonFloss and Mill Hill glass seed beads.

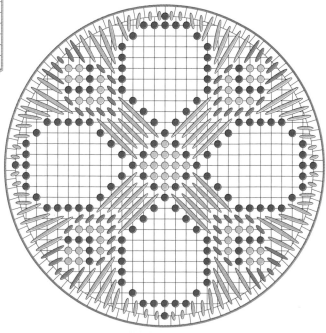

Round Box Lid & Bottom
Stitch lid only
Bottom will remain unstitched

COLOR KEY
ROUND BOX

Ribbon Floss	Yards
Smokey blue #142F-7	4
Soft pink #142F-11	8½

Glass Seed Beads
- Frosted pink parfait #62048
- Frosted denim #62043

Color numbers given are for Rhode Island Textile RibbonFloss and Mill Hill glass seed beads.

Floral Sachet

Give a gift that keeps on giving beautiful aroma! Stitch this floral potpourri sachet
as a special gift for your mother, grandmother, aunt, sister or cherished friend.

Skill Level: Beginner

Materials

- 1 sheet white 7-count plastic canvas
- Uniek Needloft plastic canvas yarn as listed in color key
- 22" ¼"-wide white satin ribbon
- White netting
- Potpourri

Instructions

1. Cut plastic canvas according to graph, cutting holes out for front only. Cut two pieces of netting to fit sachet front and back; do not cut front openings in netting.

2. Continental Stitch front. Add French Knots when background stitching is completed.

3. Place netting on backside of front and back pieces. With white, Whipstitch back to front, stitching through edges of netting and filling with potpourri before closing.

4. Cut an 8" length from white satin ribbon. Glue ends to center top of front, forming a loop for hanging. Tie remaining ribbon in a bow and glue to center top of front, covering loop ends. Trim bow tails as desired.

—Design by Carol Nartowicz

COLOR KEY	
Plastic Canvas Yarn	**Yards**
▨ Baby pink #08	1
☐ Straw #19	2
▦ Christmas green #28	1
▪ Watermelon #55	2
▨ Bright purple #64	2
╱ White #41 Whipstitching	4
○ Straw #19 French Knot	
● Bright purple #64 French Knot	
Color numbers given are for Uniek Needloft plastic canvas yarn.	

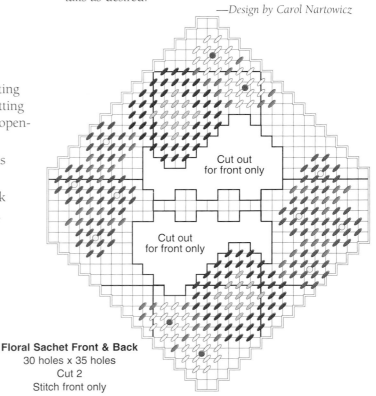

Floral Sachet Front & Back
30 holes x 35 holes
Cut 2
Stitch front only

Cut out for front only

Cut out for front only

Michael & Sarah

Wedding Favors

What bride wouldn't appreciate the gift of your time? As a special gift to her, why not stitch her wedding favors? Wedding Ring Candy Tags can be stitched in about 15 minutes. For the wedding party table, Cream Keepsakes, including a special place card and mini gift box, make memorable favors each special guest can take home.

Wedding Ring Candy Tags

Skill Level: Beginner

Materials
- ¼ sheet white 7-count plastic canvas
- Small amount clear 7-count plastic canvas
- Uniek Needloft plastic canvas yarn as listed in color key
- Fusible fleece
- 2 (15") lengths each ⅛"-wide and ¼"-wide satin ribbon to match wedding colors
- Clear plastic wrap
- Chocolate kisses

Project Note
Materials and instructions given are for two candy tag wedding favors.

Instructions
1. Cut plastic canvas according to graphs (page 99). Cut two pieces fusible fleece using plastic canvas heart as a template.

2. Place one piece fusible fleece between two hearts. Whipstitch hearts together with white. Repeat with remaining fleece and hearts.

3. Overlap one ring where indicated on graph and tack together. Wrap yellow yarn around ring following graph. Repeat with remaining three rings.

4. For one favor, cut one piece plastic wrap. Place chocolate kisses in center of plastic wrap. Using photo as a guide, wrap plastic wrap around kisses. Center one length of ⅛" ribbon on one length of ¼" ribbon; tie ribbon around plastic wrap and bring ends through holes indicated on heart graph. Tie ribbon in a bow. Glue two rings to heart below bow. Repeat with remaining favor.

—Design by Carol Nartowicz

Cream Keepsakes

Skill Level: Intermediate

Materials
- ½ sheet 7-count plastic canvas
- 2 (3") 7-count plastic canvas heart shapes by Darice
- Uniek Needloft plastic canvas yarn as listed in color key
- 3-ply lamé thread by Westrim Crafts as listed in color key
- 1 yard ⅝"-wide ivory pleated ribbon trim
- Gold ribbon roses: 3 large and 1 small
- Rose leaf clusters:
  2 small 3-leaf clusters
  1 small 2-leaf cluster
- 3⅜" x 2" name card
- Tacky glue

Mini Gift Box
1. Cut two lid sides, two box sides and outer rim from one heart for box bottom from plastic canvas according to graphs (page 99). Box bottom will remain unstitched. Second heart will remain uncut for lid top.

2. Stitch pieces with white yarn following graphs. Using double strand gold thread, work Backstitches over completed background stitching.

3. Using white through step 4, with right sides together, Whipstitch two short edges of box sides together. Bring sides down and around; with wrong sides together, Whipstitch remaining short edges together. Repeat for lid sides.

4. Overcast top edges of box sides and bottom edges of lid sides. Whipstitch box sides to box bottom and lid sides to lid top, easing canvas around curves.

5. Using photo as a guide through step 7, spread glue around unstitched edge of lid top. Beginning at bottom point, press pleated ribbon onto glue, easing around curves; cut off excess ribbon. Secure with pins until dry.

6. Spread glue around top of lid sides. Starting at top of heart, press ribbon into place around sides; cut off excess ribbon. Secure with pins until dry.

7. Glue one three-leaf cluster to top of lid top. Glue one large ribbon to center of leaf cluster.

Place Card Holder
1. Cut one place card holder front, one place card

holder back, two large stand pieces and two small stand pieces from plastic canvas according to graphs. Place card holder back and stand pieces will remain unstitched.

2. Stitch front with white yarn following graph. Using 2 strands gold thread, work Backstitches over completed background stitching.

3. Using white through step 4, Overcast inside edges of front. Whipstitch one short edge of one large stand to one short edge on one small stand from blue dot to blue dot. Repeat with remaining stand pieces.

4. Whipstitch back to front around side and bottom edges, Whipstitching small stand pieces to bottom edge from red dot to red dot as indicated on graphs.

5. Using photo as a guide through step 6, spread glue around unstitched outside edge of front. Beginning at bottom edge, press pleated ribbon onto glue, easing around corners; cut off excess ribbon. Secure with pins until dry.

6. Glue remaining three-leaf cluster to lower left corner. Glue the two-leaf cluster to upper right corner. Glue remaining two large ribbon roses to center of three-leaf cluster and small ribbon rose to center of two-leaf cluster.

7. Place name card in top opening. Place tabs on large stand pieces into slots on back.

—Designs by Ruby Thacker

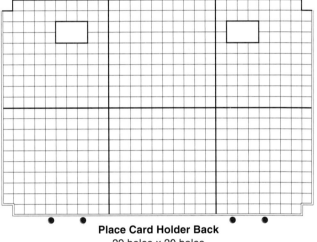

Place Card Holder Back
29 holes x 20 holes
Cut 1
Do not stitch

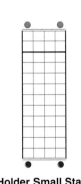

Holder Small Stand
4 holes x 12 holes
Cut 2
Do not stitch

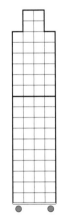

Holder Large Stand
4 holes x 18 holes
Cut 2
Do not stitch

COLOR KEY	
CREAM KEEPSAKES	
Plastic Canvas Yarn	**Yards**
☐ White #41	19
3-Ply Lamé Thread	
⟋ Gold 2-strand Backstitch	10
Color numbers given are for Uniek Needloft plastic canvas yarn.	

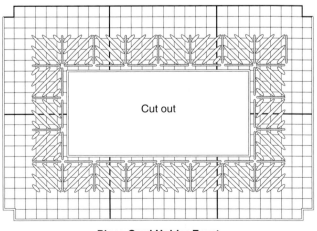

Place Card Holder Front
29 holes x 20 holes
Cut 1

COLOR KEY
WEDDING RING CANDY TAGS

Plastic Canvas Yarn	Yards
☐ Yellow #57	4
⁄ White #41 Whipstitching	5
○ Attach ribbon	

Color numbers given are for Uniek Needloft plastic canvas yarn.

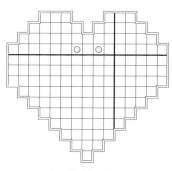

Candy Tag Heart
15 holes x 14 holes
Cut 4 from white

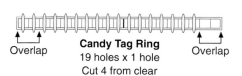

Candy Tag Ring
19 holes x 1 hole
Cut 4 from clear

Overlap   Overlap

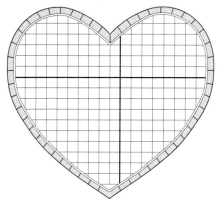

Gift Box Bottom
Cut 1
Do not stitch

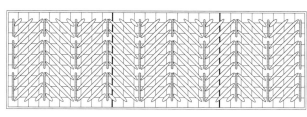

Gift Box Side
28 holes x 9 holes
Cut 2

Gift Box Lid Top
Stitch 1

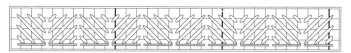

Gift Box Lid Side
31 holes x 4 holes
Cut 2

Baby Love

Delight the mother-to-be with these wonderful baby shower gifts and favors! Diaper Candy Cups, a sweet party favor, are just the right size for filling with mints or nuts. Bee Quiet and Sleepy Baby door hangers are gifts every new mother is sure to appreciate, and Baby Bunny Blocks make a sweet decoration for the nursery.

Baby Bunny Blocks

Skill Level: Beginner

Materials

- ½ sheet 7-count plastic canvas
- Uniek Needloft plastic canvas yarn as listed in color key
- #16 tapestry needle
- 1 each 1¼" blue, white and pink flocked bunnies
- Hot-glue gun

Instructions

1. Cut plastic canvas according to graphs. Cut 12 (10-hole x 10-hole) squares for remaining block sides.

2. Continental Stitch pieces following graphs. Continental Stitch four of the remaining sides with pink, four with sail blue and four with lilac.

3. Using photo as a guide and using white through step 5, for first block, Whipstitch sides together as follows: pink with heart on left side of lilac with "B," solid pink on right side of lilac with "B," solid lilac next to the two pink, and solid sail blue on top and bottom. Glue blue bunny on top, facing the "B" side.

4. Whipstitch second block sides together as follows: "A" on left side of pink with "B," solid pink on left side of "A," solid blue next to the solid pink and pink with "B," and solid lilac on top and bottom. Glue white bunny on top facing the "A, B" corner.

5. Whipstitch third block sides together as follows: sail blue with heart on right side of "Y," solid sail blue on left side of "Y," solid lilac next to the two sail blue, and solid pink on top and bottom. Glue pink bunny on top, facing the "Y" side.

—Design by Angie Arickx

Diaper Candy Cups

Skill Level: Beginner

Materials

- 1½ sheets 7-count plastic canvas
- Uniek Needloft plastic canvas yarn as listed in color key
- 4 (8") squares fusible fleece
- Monofilament
- Hot-glue gun

Instructions

1. Cut plastic canvas according to graphs. Cut four 10-hole x 9-hole pieces for candy cup bottoms. Fronts, backs, sides and bottoms will remain unstitched.

2. Stitch one diaper pin as graphed. Stitch remaining three pins replacing baby pink with baby green on one, with straw on another and with sail blue on the final pin. Overcast pins following graph.

3. With white, Whipstitch one front, one back and two sides together, then stitch one bottom to front, back and sides. Repeat with remaining three candy cups.

4. Place one cup on one fusible fleece square. Fold fleece up and over top edges of front and back. Bring sides up, folding corners to front and back to resemble diaper; fold top of fleece over top edges of cups. Tack fleece in place with monofilament. Trim ends inside basket as necessary. Repeat with remaining cups.

5. Glue one pin to front of each cup.

—*Design by Carol Nartowicz*

COLOR KEY
DIAPER CANDY CUPS

Plastic Canvas Yarn	Yards
☐ Baby pink #08	1
Straw #19	1
Baby green #26	1
Sail blue #35	1
∕ Silver #37 Overcasting	3
∕ White #41 Overcasting and Whipstitching	4

Color numbers given are for Uniek Needloft plastic canvas yarn.

Diaper Candy Cup Front & Back
14 holes x 14 holes
Cut 8
Do not stitch

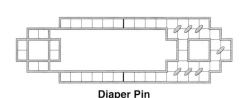

Diaper Pin
20 holes x 6 holes
Cut 4
Stitch 1 as graphed
Stitch 1 replacing baby pink with baby green,
1 replacing baby pink with straw,
1 replacing baby pink with sail blue

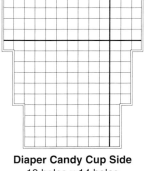

Diaper Candy Cup Side
13 holes x 14 holes
Cut 8
Do not stitch

COLOR KEY
BABY BUNNY BLOCKS

Plastic Canvas Yarn	Yards
■ Pink #07	9
■ Sail blue #35	9
☐ White #41	15
■ Lilac #45	9

Color numbers given are for Uniek Needloft plastic canvas yarn.

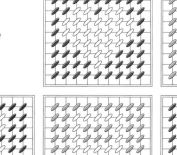
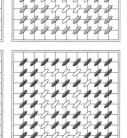
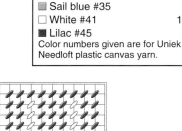
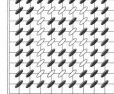
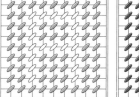
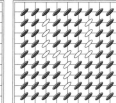

Baby Bunny Block Sides
10 holes x 10 holes
Cut 1 each

Bee Quiet

Skill Level: Beginner

Materials

- 1 sheet 7-count plastic canvas
- Uniek Needloft plastic canvas yarn as listed in color key

- DMC 6-strand embroidery floss as listed in color key
- 1 yard ¼"-wide pink satin ribbon

Instructions

1. Cut plastic canvas according to graph.

2. Continental Stitch and Overcast piece following graph. Work pearl cotton embroidery when background stitching is completed.

3. Glue center of ribbon to back of head. Tie ends in a bow around doorknob, trimming ends as desired.

—Design by Michele Wilcox

COLOR KEY	
BEE QUIET	
Plastic Canvas Yarn	**Yards**
■ Black #00	5
☐ Yellow #57	4
Uncoded areas are white #41 Continental Stitches	16
╱ White #41 Overcasting	
6-Strand Embroidery Floss	
╱ Blue #799 Backstitch	2
╱ Willow green #3346 Backstitch	2
○ Very light topaz #727 French Knot	1
◐ Salmon #760 French Knot	2
● Blue #799 French Knot	
✍ Willow green #3346 Lazy Daisy	
Color numbers given are for Uniek Needloft plastic canvas yarn and DMC 6-strand embroidery floss.	

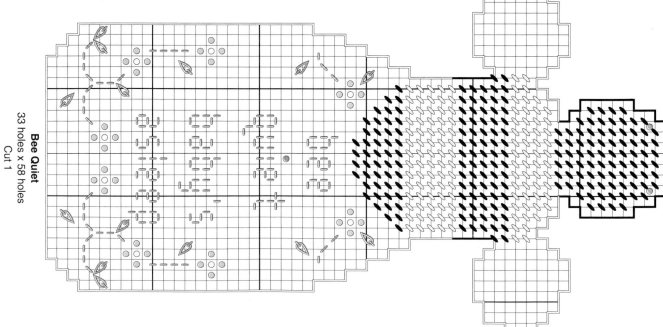

Bee Quiet
33 holes x 58 holes
Cut 1

Sleepy Baby

Skill Level: Beginner

Materials

- ¾ sheet 7-count plastic canvas
- J. & P. Coats plastic canvas yarn Article E.46 as listed in color key
- Anchor 6-strand embroidery floss by Coats & Clark as listed in color key
- Brown curly doll hair
- ¼" pink pompon
- Thick tacky craft glue

Instructions

1. Cut plastic canvas according to graphs.

2. Stitch pieces following graphs. Overcast hanger with Olympic blue, moon with tangerine and baby with paddy green and sea coral following graphs. Work embroidery with yarn and 6 strands floss when background stitching is completed.

3. Using photo as a guide throughout, glue pompon to cheek and small amount of hair to head. Glue baby to moon and moon to hanger.

—Design by Nancy Marshall

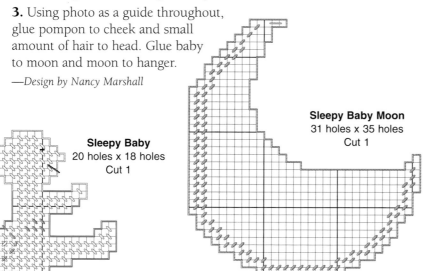

Sleepy Baby
20 holes x 18 holes
Cut 1

Sleepy Baby Moon
31 holes x 35 holes
Cut 1

COLOR KEY	
SLEEPY BABY	
Plastic Canvas Yarn	**Yards**
☐ Yellow #230	4
☐ Sea coral #246	1½
■ Tangerine #253	3½
☐ Emerald green #676	1
■ Paddy green #686	1
■ Olympic blue #849	24
Uncoded area on moon is orange #245 Continental Stitches	4
╱ Orange #245 Straight Stitch	
╱ Paddy green #686 Backstitch	
6-Strand Embroidery Floss	
╱ Bright Christmas red #46 Straight Stitch	¼
╱ Black #403 Straight Stitch	¼
Color numbers given are for J. & P. Coats plastic canvas yarn and Anchor 6-strand embroidery floss.	

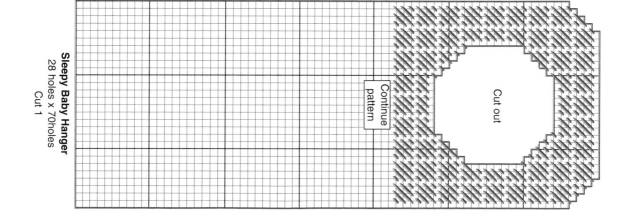

Sleepy Baby Hanger
28 holes x 70holes
Cut 1

Continue pattern

Cut out

Kid-Pleasing Projects

Always on the lookout for cute, yet quick-to-stitch gifts for kids? Look no further! The following collection of projects will give you more than a dozen great gift ideas, plus items you can use to teach your youngster how to stitch his or her own plastic canvas projects!

Elephant Crayon Holder

Stitch this delightful project for your aspiring artist! This adorable elephant crayon holder stands on its own and holds more than a dozen crayons on its back!

Skill Level: Intermediate

Materials
- 1 sheet 7-count plastic canvas
- 2 (4½") plastic canvas radial circles
- 2 (3") plastic canvas radial circles
- Spinrite plastic canvas yarn as listed in color key
- DMC #3 pearl cotton as listed in color key
- #16 tapestry needle
- 2 (10mm) round black cabochons
- Hot-glue gun

Project Note
Use 4½" circles for elephant body and 3" circles for elephant head.

Cutting
1. Cut canvas according to graphs. Do not cut circles.

2. Cut one 21-hole x 9-hole piece for pocket bottom, one 21-hole x 14-hole piece for pocket front, one 21-hole x 14-hole piece for pocket back and two 9-hole x 14-hole pieces for pocket short sides. Pocket pieces, tusks and four leg pieces will remain unstitched.

Stitching
1. Using silver gray through step 7, Cross Stitch across center row of holes on one 3" circle. Straight Stitch around circle from the center row of holes to the third row of holes.

2. Continue Straight Stitching around circle from the third row of holes to the fifth row, from the fifth to the seventh and from the seventh to the ninth, which is the outside row of holes, using two stitches per hole as necessary to cover canvas. Repeat for remaining 3" circle.

3. Follow steps 2 and 3 for stitching the 4½" circles, continuing stitch pattern from the ninth row of holes to the 11th row of holes and from the 11th to the 13th, which is the outside row of holes.

4. Whipstitch pocket front and back to pocket sides, then Whipstitch pocket bottom to pocket front, back and sides.

5. Stitch remaining pieces following graphs, reversing one trunk before stitching. For ear fronts, stitch two ear pieces in pale pink following graph, reversing one before stitching. For ear backs, Continental Stitch remaining two ear pieces in silver gray, reversing one before stitching.

6. With wrong sides together, Whipstitch one ear front to one ear back. Repeat with remaining ear pieces. Whipstitch one unstitched leg to backside of one stitched leg. Repeat with remaining leg pieces. Whipstitch wrong sides of trunk pieces together.

7. Work black pearl cotton French Knots for toes, reversing French Knot pattern on two legs. Overcast tusks with white, reversing one tusk before Overcasting.

Assembly

1. Using silver gray through step 2, Whipstitch one long edge on body side to body circle, using two stitches per hole as necessary in body when easing side around circle. Whipstitch remaining body circle to remaining long edge on body side.

2. Whipstitch head sides to head circle following instructions in step 1 for body pieces. Overcast remaining head edges.

3. For tail, cut two 12" lengths of silver gray yarn. Thread both lengths through needle. Insert needle from front to back through one of the holes indicated on body side graph, then bring needle from back to front through remaining hole indicated on body side graph. Braid yarn for approximately 1", then tie in a knot; cut off ends.

4. Insert pocket into body. Using silver gray throughout, Whipstitch top edges of pocket sides to short edges of body sides. Overcast remaining edges of body circles.

5. Using photo as a guide through step 6, insert head end of body into opening on head so that top edge of head opening rests on top edge of body side and pocket; glue head in place.

6. Glue legs to body, making sure they are even on both sides so body does not rock. Glue ears, tusks, trunk and cabochons to head.

—Design by Vicki Blizzard

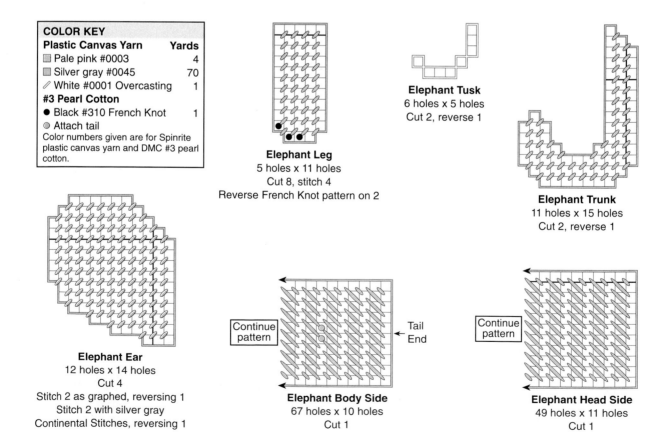

COLOR KEY

Plastic Canvas Yarn	Yards
▨ Pale pink #0003	4
☐ Silver gray #0045	70
⁄ White #0001 Overcasting	1

#3 Pearl Cotton

● Black #310 French Knot	1
○ Attach tail	

Color numbers given are for Spinrite plastic canvas yarn and DMC #3 pearl cotton.

Elephant Tusk
6 holes x 5 holes
Cut 2, reverse 1

Elephant Leg
5 holes x 11 holes
Cut 8, stitch 4
Reverse French Knot pattern on 2

Elephant Trunk
11 holes x 15 holes
Cut 2, reverse 1

Elephant Ear
12 holes x 14 holes
Cut 4
Stitch 2 as graphed, reversing 1
Stitch 2 with silver gray
Continental Stitches, reversing 1

Continue pattern

Tail End

Elephant Body Side
67 holes x 10 holes
Cut 1

Continue pattern

Elephant Head Side
49 holes x 11 holes
Cut 1

Sunshine Teddy Bear

Dress up a cuddly teddy bear in this sweet baby yellow outfit including a top,
easy-to-sew skirt, parasol and sandals!

Skill Level: Intermediate

Materials
- 1 sheet 7-count plastic canvas
- 8" plastic canvas circle

- Uniek Needloft plastic canvas yarn as listed in color key
- 10" ¼"-diameter dowel
- Yellow craft paint
- 31" ⅛"-wide yellow satin ribbon

- 2 (13mm x 11mm) white wooden beads with ¼" hole
- ½" round adhesive-backed hook-and-loop fasteners
- 2 #1 snaps
- Sewing needle
- Yellow sewing thread
- 5½" x 25" piece yellow cotton-polyester blend fabric
- 11" ⅛"-wide elastic
- Sewing machine
- 12" teddy bear with 10" waist measurement
- Tacky glue

Purse & Parasol

1. Cut six parasol pieces, one parasol stop and one each of purse front, back, top and flap from plastic canvas following graphs (below and page 109). Parasol stop will remain unstitched.

2. Stitch purse front, back and top following graphs. Stitch parasol pieces and purse flap, working lavender roses first, then stitching baby yellow Slanting Gobelin Stitches. Work Lazy Daisy Stitches over completed background stitching.

3. Using baby yellow through step 4, Whipstitch one long edge of purse top to top edge of purse back. Whipstitch remaining long edge of purse top to top edge of purse flap. With wrong sides together, Whipstitch purse front and back together along side and bottom edges. Overcast remaining edges of purse.

4. Whipstitch side edges of parasol pieces together from blue dot to blue dot. Overcast remaining edges.

5. Cut a 7" length from yellow satin ribbon, fold in half and glue ends inside one top corner of purse. Glue or tack hook-and-loop fastener on inside of purse flap and on purse front.

6. Paint dowel with yellow craft paint. Allow to dry. Slide dowel through hole in center of parasol. Glue bead to top end. Allow to dry. Place parasol under bead. Slide unstitched stop under parasol and glue in place. Glue remaining bead to bottom end of dowel.

Vest & Sandals

1. Cut one vest back, two vest fronts, two sandal soles, two sandal heels and four sandal straps from plastic canvas according to graphs (below and page 109).

2. Using baby yellow through step 3, stitch vest following graphs, reversing one front. Overlap vest front and back pieces at sides before stitching and rotate shoulders, matching red dots, before stitching. Overcast edges.

3. Stitch sandals following graphs. Place one sole with wrong side up, then Whipstitch bottom edge of one heel around heel edge of sandal between blue hearts. Stitch one strap to each side of sandal from red heart to red heart. Overcast all remaining edges. Repeat for second sandal.

4. With sewing needle and yellow thread, sew snaps to vest front, lining up thread carefully so stitches do not show.

5. Cut remaining yellow ribbon in half. For each sandal, thread one length through holes in sandal straps and tie in a bow.

Skirt

1. With right sides facing, sew yellow fabric together along short sides. Stitch ½" hem in bottom.

2. Turn top edge under ¼"; press. Turn under again ½"; sew edge, leaving channel for elastic. Thread elastic through skirt; test fit on bear's waist. Stitch elastic to secure; stitch opening closed.

—*Design by Terry Ricioli*

COLOR KEY	
Plastic Canvas Yarn	**Yards**
▨ Lavender #05	3
☐ Baby yellow #21	50
✎ Lavender #05 Backstitch	
✐ Mermaid #53 Lazy Daisy	3
◌ Attach snap	
Color numbers given are for Uniek Needloft plastic canvas yarn.	

Purse Top
21 holes x 2 holes
Cut 1

Parasol Stop
4 holes x 4 holes
Cut 1
Do not stitch

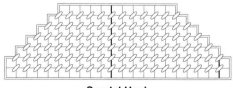

Sandal Heel
21 holes x 7 holes
Cut 2

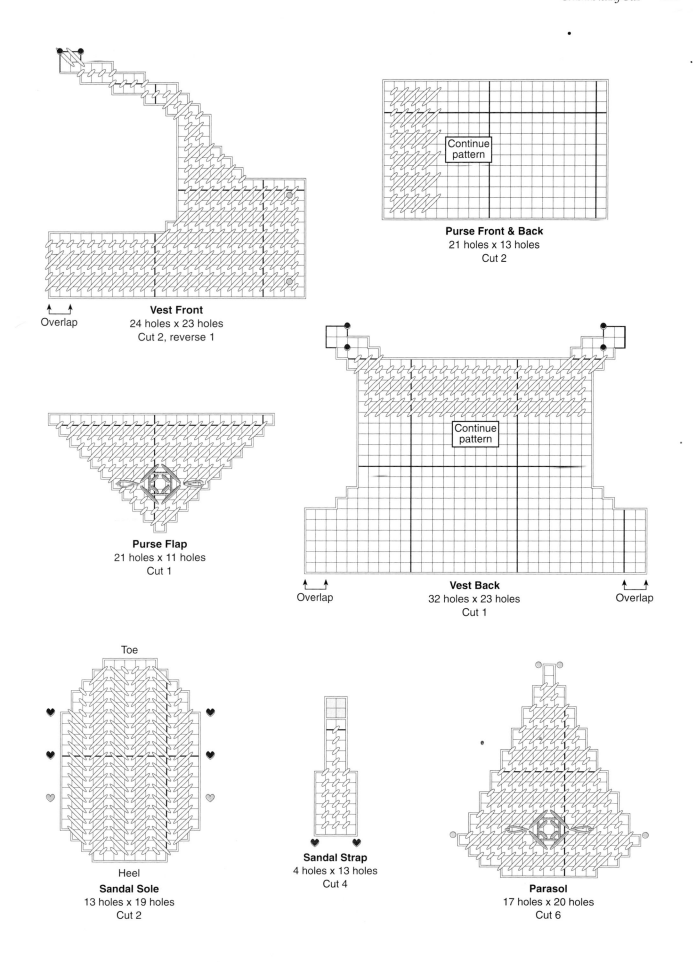

Purse Front & Back
21 holes x 13 holes
Cut 2

Continue pattern

Vest Front
24 holes x 23 holes
Cut 2, reverse 1

Overlap

Purse Flap
21 holes x 11 holes
Cut 1

Continue pattern

Vest Back
32 holes x 23 holes
Cut 1

Overlap

Overlap

Toe

Heel

Sandal Sole
13 holes x 19 holes
Cut 2

Sandal Strap
4 holes x 13 holes
Cut 4

Parasol
17 holes x 20 holes
Cut 6

Musical Teddy Bears

Toddlers will especially love their very own musical bear! Just press their tummies and listen to a pretty tune!

Skill Level: Beginner

Materials

- 1 sheet 7-count plastic canvas
- Worsted weight yarn as listed in color key
- #16 tapestry needle
- 2 music buttons
- 9" ⅜"-wide white lace
- Craft glue

Instructions

1. Cut plastic canvas according to graphs (page 111).

2. Stitch fronts following graphs, Overcasting shoulder straps and crotch areas.

3. Stitch backs following graphs, working heads entirely with tan Continental Stitches, eliminating facial features; stitch blouse and shirt backs entirely with Continental Stitches, eliminating buttons.

Overcast shoulder strap and crotch areas. **Note:** To make Whipstitching easier, leave yarn tails on hands and feet.

4. With wrong sides together, Whipstitch corresponding backs and fronts together at hands and feet. Whipstitch legs together up to hands with adjacent colors. Insert music button in each bear and push down as far as it will go. Complete Whipstitching with adjacent colors.

5. Using photo as a guide, glue lace around hem of girl bear's jumper, beginning and ending at center back.

6. For hanger, cut a 4½"–5" length of tan yarn for each bear. Thread yarn from back to front through holes indicated on graph. Tie ends in a knot to form a loop for hanging.

—Designs by Alida Macor

COLOR KEY BOY BEAR	
Worsted Weight Yarn	**Yards**
■ Blue	9
■ Tan	7
□ Yellow	5
■ Pink	½
□ White	½
■ Black	½
● Attach hanger	

COLOR KEY GIRL BEAR	
Worsted Weight Yarn	**Yards**
■ Tan	9
■ Pink	7
□ White	5
■ Black	½
● Attach hanger	

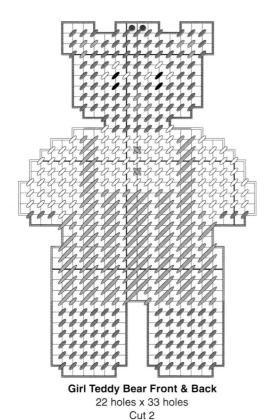

Girl Teddy Bear Front & Back
22 holes x 33 holes
Cut 2

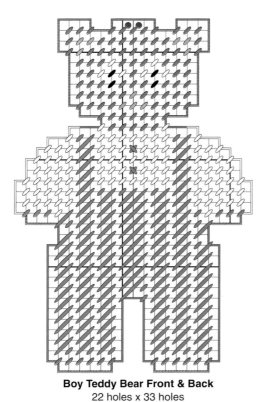

Boy Teddy Bear Front & Back
22 holes x 33 holes
Cut 2

Beary Happy

If your kids often want to help you with your plastic canvas stitching, here is the perfect project! Even young children can do a simple Running Stitch outline, or even help sew on the buttons! Everyone will be "beary happy"!

Skill Level: Beginner

Materials

- ½ sheet brown 14-count plastic canvas
- ¼ sheet white 14-count plastic canvas
- DMC 6-strand embroidery floss as listed in color key
- 5" x 2½" piece polyester batting
- 4 (½") brown buttons
- 12" ⅛"-wide red satin ribbon
- Tacky glue

Instructions

1. Cut body, legs and arms from brown plastic canvas and cloud from white plastic canvas following graphs.

2. Using 6 strands floss for all stitching, stitch ears, nose, eyes and mouth on bear body with russet. Backstitch with white around eyes.

3. Backstitch letters on cloud with bright Christmas red. Using russet on body, arms and legs and bright Christmas red on cloud, work a Running Stitch (Fig. 1) around edges of each piece following graphs or as desired, reversing one arm and one leg before stitching.

4. Using russet floss, sew one button to one arm and body where indicated on graph. Repeat for remaining arm and both legs.

5. Thread red satin ribbon from front to back through holes indicated on graph. Tie ribbon in a bow; trim tails as desired.

6. Cut two 9" lengths of bright Christmas red floss. Lay cloud above bear. Thread one length floss through hand and cloud on left side where indicated on graphs with green dots. Tie floss in a knot and then in a bow at cloud. Repeat with remaining floss on right side, making sure bear hangs evenly.

7. Glue batting to backside of cloud. Slightly pull edges for a fluffier look. Hang as desired.

—Design by Janna Britton

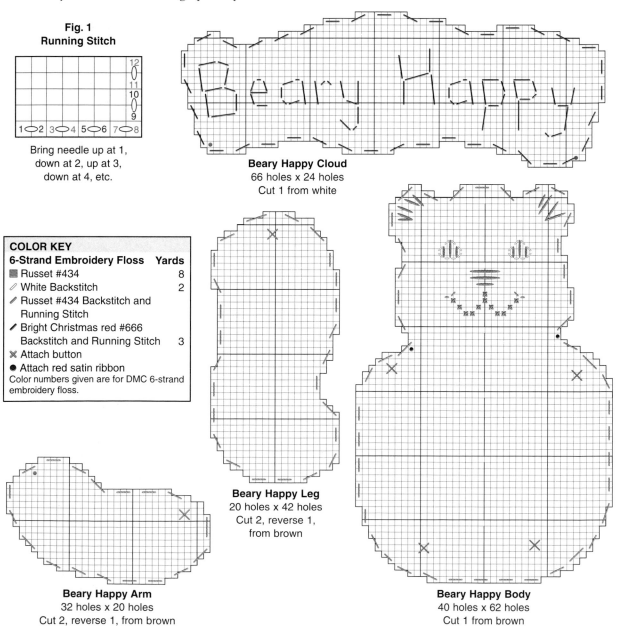

Fig. 1
Running Stitch

Bring needle up at 1,
down at 2, up at 3,
down at 4, etc.

Beary Happy Cloud
66 holes x 24 holes
Cut 1 from white

COLOR KEY
6-Strand Embroidery Floss **Yards**
▪ Russet #434   8
╱ White Backstitch   2
╱ Russet #434 Backstitch and
  Running Stitch
╱ Bright Christmas red #666
  Backstitch and Running Stitch   3
✕ Attach button
● Attach red satin ribbon
Color numbers given are for DMC 6-strand
embroidery floss.

Beary Happy Leg
20 holes x 42 holes
Cut 2, reverse 1,
from brown

Beary Happy Arm
32 holes x 20 holes
Cut 2, reverse 1, from brown

Beary Happy Body
40 holes x 62 holes
Cut 1 from brown

Magnetic Photo Frames

Show off your little sweethearts by displaying their wallet-sized photos in these colorful refrigerator magnets!

Skill Level: Beginner

Materials
All Magnets
- Uniek Needloft plastic canvas yarn as listed in color key
- DMC #3 pearl cotton as listed in color key
- #16 tapestry needle
- Hot-glue gun

Blackboard
- ¼ sheet Uniek Quick-Count 7-count plastic canvas
- 2 (2½") magnetic strips

Little Blue Roadster
- ½ sheet Uniek Quick-Count 7-count plastic canvas
- ⅛"-wide Plastic Canvas 7 Metallic Needlepoint Yarn by Rainbow Gallery as listed in color key
- 3" magnetic strip

My Heart
- ¼ sheet Uniek Quick-Count 7-count plastic canvas
- 2 (2") magnetic strips

Rainbow Superstar
- 2 (7-count) plastic canvas star shapes by Uniek
- Small amount Uniek Quick-Count 7-count plastic canvas
- 2 (1¼") magnetic strips

Blackboard

1. Cut plastic canvas according to graphs (page 115). Frame back will remain unstitched.

2. Continental Stitch frame front with black. With white pearl cotton, center and Backstitch school grade desired in blue area on graph. Work remainder of Backstitches with pearl cotton.

3. Overcast inside edges on frame front with black. Whipstitch frame front to frame back with maple.

4. Glue one magnetic strip to each short end on frame back, making sure glue does not adhere to frame front.

Little Blue Roadster

1. Cut plastic canvas according to graphs (page 115). Frame back will remain unstitched.

2. Stitch pieces following graphs. Work pearl cotton Backstitches when background stitching is completed.

3. Using royal throughout, Overcast inside edges of frame front. Overcast top edge of frame front from dot to dot. Whipstitch frame front to frame back around sides and bottom from dot to dot.

4. Overcast headlights and grille with silver and fenders and tires with adjacent colors.

5. Using photo as a guide throughout, center and glue grille to bottom edge of frame front. Glue one headlight to each side of grille. Center and glue top edge of tires behind fenders. Glue fenders and tires to frame front.

6. Glue magnetic strip to frame back, making sure glue does not adhere to frame front.

My Heart

1. Cut flowers, frame front and back and one sign as desired from plastic canvas according to graphs, cutting out opening in frame front only. Frame back will remain unstitched.

2. Continental Stitch frame front and sign with white. Work pearl cotton embroidery when background stitching is completed. Using 1 ply yarn, stitch flowers following graphs.

3. Overcast inside edges of frame front with Christmas red. Overcast sign and top edge of frame front with yellow. Overcast flowers with adjacent colors. With yellow, Whipstitch frame front to frame back around side and bottom edges.

4. Using photo as a guide throughout, glue flowers to frame front at top of stems. Glue sign to lower right-hand corner.

5. Glue magnetic strips to frame back at top and bottom edges, making sure glue does not adhere to frame front.

Rainbow Superstar

1. Cut stars and streamers according to graphs (page 116), cutting away shaded gray areas. Frame back will remain unstitched.

2. Stitch frame front. Continental Stitch streamers with Christmas red. Work pearl cotton Backstitches

when Continental Stitching is completed.

3. Using white throughout, Overcast inside edges of frame front and streamers. Overcast top edge of frame front from dot to dot. Whipstitch frame front to frame back around side and bottom edges from dot to dot.

4. Using photo as a guide, glue tops of streamers and magnetic strips to frame back, making sure glue does not adhere to frame front.

—Designs by Vicki Blizzard

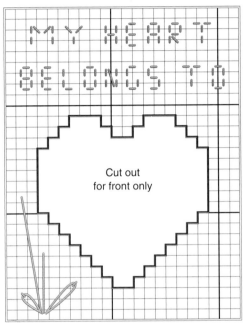

My Heart Frame Front & Back
22 holes x 29 holes
Cut 2, stitch 1

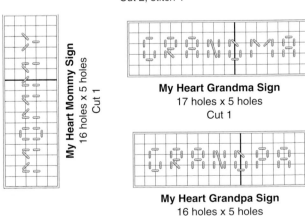

My Heart Mommy Sign
16 holes x 5 holes
Cut 1

My Heart Grandma Sign
17 holes x 5 holes
Cut 1

My Heart Grandpa Sign
16 holes x 5 holes
Cut 1

My Heart Daddy Sign
13 holes x 5 holes
Cut 1

My Heart Flowers
3 holes x 3 holes
Cut 1 each

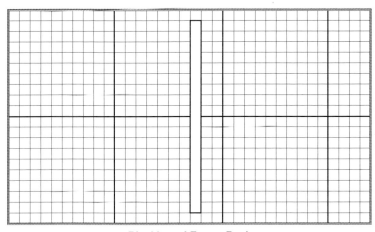

Blackboard Frame Back
34 holes x 20 holes
Cut 1
Do not stitch

COLOR KEY
BLACKBOARD

Plastic Canvas Yarn	Yards
Uncoded area is black #00 Continental Stitches	9
✎ Black #00 Overcasting	
✎ Maple #13 Overcasting	2
#3 Pearl Cotton	
⟋ Snow white Backstitch	1
⟋ Light lemon #445 Backstitch	½
⟋ Very light blue #827 Backstitch	½
⟋ Light Nile green #955 Backstitch	½

Color numbers given are for Uniek Needloft
plastic canvas yarn and DMC #3 pearl cotton.

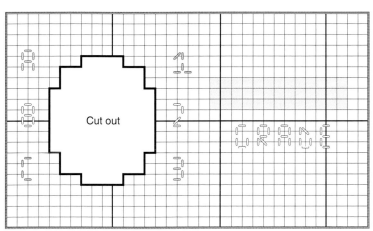

Blackboard Frame Front
34 holes x 20 holes
Cut 1

Blackboard School Grades

Roadster Grille
9 holes x 5 holes
Cut 1

Roadster Headlight
4 holes x 4 holes
Cut 2

Roadster Fender
7 holes x 3 holes
Cut 2

Roadster Tire
3 holes x 7 holes
Cut 2

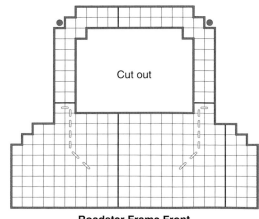

Roadster Frame Back
23 holes x 18 holes
Cut 1
Do not stitch

COLOR KEY
MY HEART

Plastic Canvas Yarn	Yards
■ Christmas red #02	1
☐ Yellow #57	2
Uncoded areas are white #41 Continental Stitches	7
#3 Pearl Cotton	
⟋ Kelly green #701 Backstitch	2
⟋ Medium blue #797 Backstitch	2
◉ Kelly green #701 Lazy Daisy	

Color numbers given are for Uniek Needloft
plastic canvas yarn and DMC #3 pearl cotton.

COLOR KEY
LITTLE BLUE ROADSTER

Plastic Canvas Yarn	Yards
■ Black #00	1
■ Royal #32	6
☐ White #41	1
Uncoded area on frame front is royal #32 Continental Stitches	
⅛ " Metallic Needlepoint Yarn	
☐ Silver #PC2	2
#3 Pearl Cotton	
⟋ Snow white Backstitch	1
⟋ Black #310 Backstitch	1

Color numbers given are for Uniek Needloft
plastic canvas yarn, Rainbow Gallery Plastic
Canvas 7 Needlepoint Yarn and DMC #3 pearl
cotton.

Roadster Frame Front
23 holes x 19 holes
Cut 1

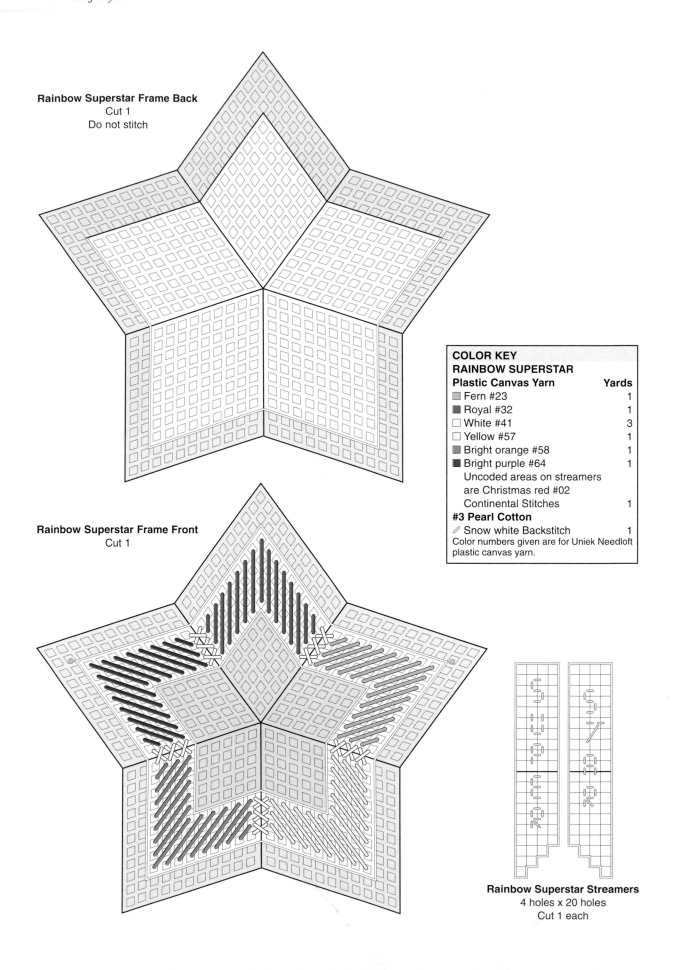

Rainbow Superstar Frame Back
Cut 1
Do not stitch

Rainbow Superstar Frame Front
Cut 1

COLOR KEY	
RAINBOW SUPERSTAR	
Plastic Canvas Yarn	**Yards**
▨ Fern #23	1
◼ Royal #32	1
☐ White #41	3
☐ Yellow #57	1
▨ Bright orange #58	1
◼ Bright purple #64	1
Uncoded areas on streamers are Christmas red #02 Continental Stitches	1
#3 Pearl Cotton	
✎ Snow white Backstitch	1
Color numbers given are for Uniek Needloft plastic canvas yarn.	

Rainbow Superstar Streamers
4 holes x 20 holes
Cut 1 each

Rainy-Day Bank

Save up for a rainy-day trip to the movies or arcade with this eye-catching coin bank.

Skill Level: Beginner

Materials

- 1 sheet 7-count plastic canvas
- J. & P. Coats 4-ply craft yarn Art. E.48 as listed in color key
- Kreinik ⅛" Ribbon as listed in color key
- #16 tapestry needle
- Orange pipe cleaner
- Tacky craft glue

Instructions

1. Cut plastic canvas according to graphs (pages 118 and 119). Cut one 33-hole x 28-hole piece for bank bottom. Bank bottom will remain unstitched.

2. Stitch pieces following graphs. Work pearl ribbon Lazy Daisy Stitches over background stitching.

3. Overcast around sides and top of umbrella with yellow; bottom edge will remain unstitched. Overcast inside edges of opening on bank top with blue jewel. Following graphs, Whipstitch front, left, back and right sides together with blue jewel and white, then Whipstitch sides to top and bottom.

4. Using photo as a guide throughout, bend top end of pipe cleaner; center and glue to back of umbrella so bent end shows slightly above top edge of umbrella. Bend bottom end of pipe cleaner in a "U," forming umbrella handle. Glue umbrella to bank front side.

5. To remove money from bank, either work it through coin slot with a butter knife or snip 1" of Whipstitching on bottom back edge; Whipstitch closed when money is removed.

—*Design by Judi Kauffman*

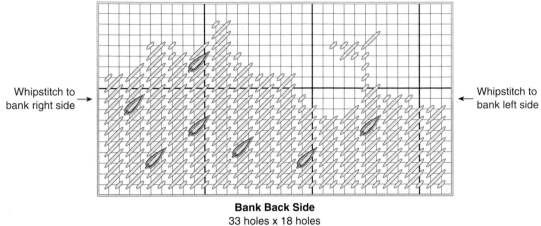

Bank Back Side
33 holes x 18 holes
Cut 1

Whipstitch to
bank right side →

← Whipstitch to
bank left side

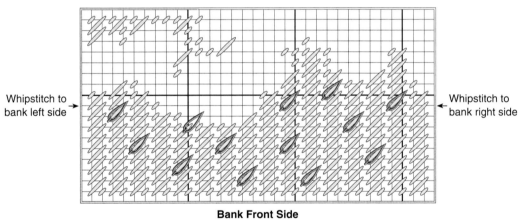

Bank Front Side
33 holes x 18 holes
Cut 1

Whipstitch to
bank left side →

← Whipstitch to
bank right side

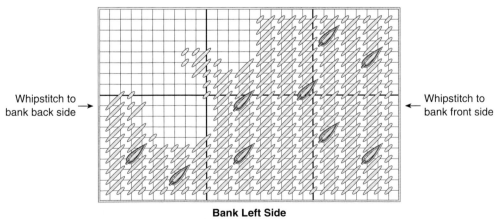

Bank Left Side
28 holes x 18 holes
Cut 1

Whipstitch to →
bank back side

← Whipstitch to
bank front side

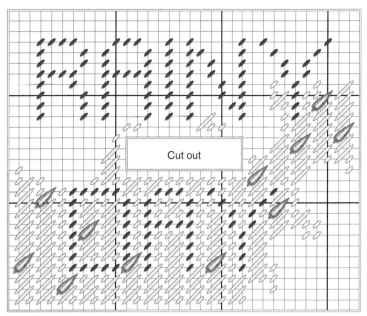

Bank Top
33 holes x 28 holes
Cut 1

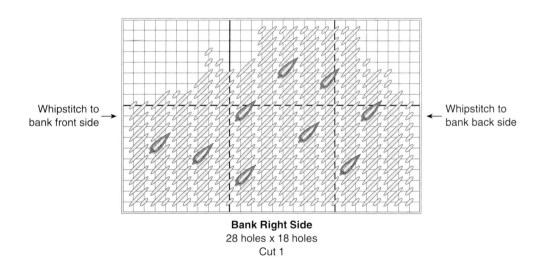

Whipstitch to
bank front side →

← Whipstitch to
bank back side

Bank Right Side
28 holes x 18 holes
Cut 1

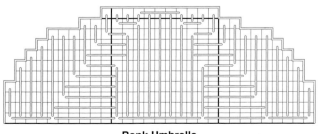

Bank Umbrella
29 holes x 11 holes
Cut 1

COLOR KEY

4-Ply Craft Yarn	Yards
☐ Blue jewel #818	30
■ Olympic blue #849	3
Uncoded areas are white	
#1 Continental Stitches	17
⟋ White #1 Whipstitching	
⟋ Yellow #230 Straight Stitch	3
and Overcasting	
⅛ " Ribbon	
⟠ Pearl #032 Lazy Daisy	5½

Color numbers given are for J. & P. Coats
4-ply craft yarn and Kreinik ⅛" Ribbon.

Playing Card Set

Teaching kids to play "Go Fish" or "Concentration" is more fun and exciting when the kids have their very own sparkling card case and score-keeping pad!

Skill Level: Intermediate

Materials

- 1 sheet 7-count plastic canvas
- Uniek Needloft plastic canvas yarn as listed in color key
- ⅛"-wide Plastic Canvas 7 Metallic Needlepoint Yarn by Rainbow Gallery as listed in color key
- 3" x 5" spiral-top note pad
- Pencil

Instructions

1. Cut plastic canvas according to graphs (page 121). Cut two 27-hole x 6-hole pieces for lid short sides. Cut one 36-hole x 25-hole piece for box bottom, two 36-hole x 6-hole pieces for box long sides and three 25-hole x 6-hole pieces for box short sides and divider.

2. Stitch pieces following graphs. Continental Stitch lid short sides with white. Stitch border only on score pad holder back. Work black Straight Stitches over completed background stitching. Box bottom, sides and divider will remain unstitched.

3. Using white throughout, Whipstitch box sides together, then Whipstitch sides to box bottom.

Whipstitch divider to middle bar of box bottom and middle bar of box long sides. Whipstitch lid sides together.

4. Using gold through step 7, Whipstitch lid sides to lid top. Overcast bottom edges of lid sides.

5. For score pad holder, Overcast pencil holder long edges. Whipstitch top edge of front to one long edge of top piece. Whipstitch remaining long edge of top piece to top edge of back.

6. Whipstitch sides to front and top pieces. Overcast bottom edges of front and sides.

7. Overcast side and bottom edges of back piece, Whipstitching sides to back and both short edges of pencil holder to back from dot to dot where indicated on graph while Overcasting.

8. Insert note pad and pencil into holder.

—*Designs by Kathleen Kennebeck*

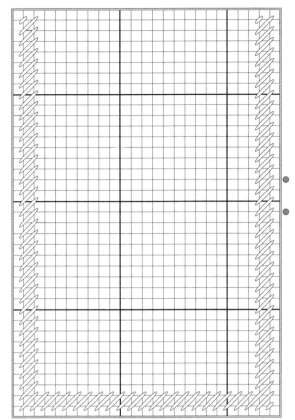

Score Pad Holder Back
25 holes x 38 holes
Cut 1

Pencil Holder
12 holes x 3 holes
Cut 1

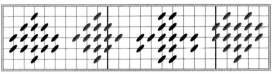

Score Pad Holder Front
25 holes x 6 holes
Cut 1

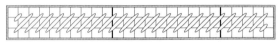

Score Pad Holder Top
25 holes x 3 holes
Cut 1

COLOR KEY

Plastic Canvas Yarn	**Yards**
■ Black #00	4
■ Red #01	4
☐ White #41	15

Uncoded areas are white #41
Continental Stitches
✔ Black #00 Straight Stitch

⅛" Metallic Needlepoint Yarn

☐ Gold #PC 1	8

Color numbers given are for Uniek Needloft
plastic canvas yarn and Rainbow Gallery
Plastic Canvas 7 Metallic Needlepoint Yarn.

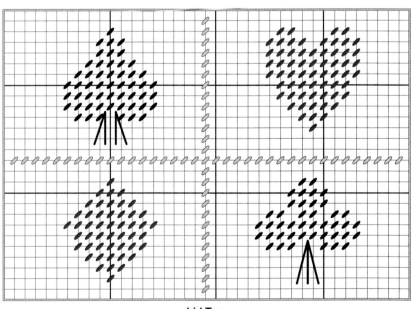

Lid Top
38 holes x 27 holes
Cut 1

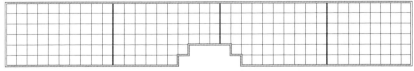

Lid Large Side
38 holes x 6 holes
Cut 2

Score Pad Holder Side
3 holes x 6 holes
Cut 2

Heart Danglers

Girls like sugar 'n spice and everything nice, like ponytail or shoe danglers! Stitch a pair in colors to match her favorite outfit!

Skill Level: Intermediate

Materials
One Dangler

- Small amount 7-count plastic canvas
- Worsted weight yarn as listed in color key
- #18 tapestry needle
- Needle-nose pliers

COLOR KEY	
Worsted Weight Yarn	**Yards**
Amethyst	4

Heart Dangler
5 holes x 5 holes
Cut 8

Project Notes

Instructions and graph given are for one dangler, though three are shown in photo.

Any color may be used for danglers. Samples used amethyst, bright pink and turquoise.

Instructions

1. Cut eight hearts from plastic canvas according to graph.

2. Following graph, stack two hearts together and stitch as one with a 12" length of yarn. Repeat with remaining hearts for a total of four hearts.

3. Thread needle to center of 40" strand of yarn. With wrong sides together and beginning at bottom, Whipstitch two hearts together with the doubled strand. Upon completion, bring needle up through center bottom of heart through center top of heart, using needle-nose pliers to pull needle through; trim ends.

4. Repeat for remaining two hearts, trimming only one strand yarn at top of heart. Thread remaining strand through first heart from top to bottom, leaving approximately 4" between hearts for shoe danglers and a longer length as desired for ponytails. Stitch around edge at bottom to secure; trim off end even with surface.

—Design by E. Wayne Fox

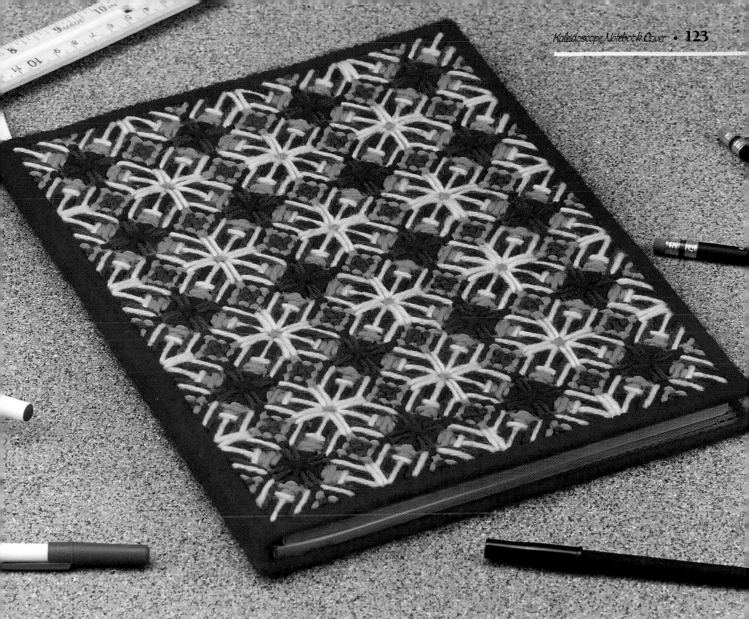

Kaleidoscope Notebook Cover

Try your hand at a variety of interesting stitches while making this colorful notebook cover!

Skll Level: Advanced

Materials

- 2 sheets clear 7-count plastic canvas
- 1 sheet red 7-count plastic canvas
- Plastic canvas yarn as listed in color key
- 8½" x 10½" piece red felt
- Hot-glue gun

Instructions

1. Cut plastic canvas according to graphs (page 124). Cut one 58-hole x 72-hole piece from red plastic canvas for back cover and one 52-hole x 72-hole piece from clear plastic canvas for inset.

Back cover and inset will remain unstitched.

2. Stitch pieces following graph, working one color at a time for front cover and beginning with blue.

3. Using red through step 4, Whipstitch one long edge of spine to one long edge of front. Whipstitch remaining long edge of spine to one long edge of back.

4. Place inset inside back cover so outside edges match. Whipstitch inset to back cover along outside edges only, Overcasting remaining cover edges while Whipstitching.

5. Trim felt to fit inside front cover; glue in place. Slip back cover of spiral notebook into inset.

—*Design by Linda L. Smith*

Cover Front
58 holes x 72 holes
Cut 1 from clear

COLOR KEY	
Plastic Canvas Yarn	**Yards**
■ Red	50
■ Blue	30
□ Yellow	25
■ Green	23

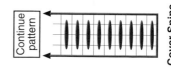

Cover Spine
4 holes x 72 holes
Cut 1 from clear

Continue pattern

Quiet Time Doorknob Hangers

Keep the house still and quiet by letting the family know when a youngster is studying or Baby is sleeping.

Study Time

Skill Level: Beginner

Materials

- 1 sheet Uniek Quick-Count 7-count plastic canvas
- Uniek Needloft plastic canvas yarn as listed in color key
- Kreinik Heavy (#32) Braid as listed in color key

Instructions

1. Cut hanger front and back from plastic canvas according to graph (page 126). Hanger back will remain unstitched.

2. Stitch front following graph. Work French Knot and Backstitches over completed background stitching.

3. Whipstitch back to front along inside and outside edges with white and maple following graph.

—*Design by Mary T. Cosgrove*

Baby Is Sleeping

Skill Level: Beginner

Materials

- 1 sheet 7-count plastic canvas
- J. & P. Coats 4-ply craft yarn Article E.48 as listed in color key
- #16 tapestry needle
- Small amount Kreinik Fine (#8) Braid: gold #002
- Sewing needle
- Ceramic buttons by Mill Hill Products from Gay Bowles Sales, Inc.:

  2 angels #86011

  3 gold stars #86016
- 6½" x 8½" piece lavender felt
- Tacky craft glue

Instructions

1. Cut hanger from plastic canvas according to graph (page 126).

2. Continental Stitch piece following graph. Overcast inside and outside edges with lavender.

3. With sewing needle and gold braid, attach angel and star buttons to finished piece where indicated on graph.

—*Design by Judi Kauffman*

COLOR KEY
BABY IS SLEEPING

4-Ply Craft Yarn	Yards
Sea coral #246	7
Lavender #584	12
Light seafoam #683	6
Grenadine #730	3
Uncoded area is white #1 Continental Stitches	16
● Attach angel button	
● Attach star button	

Color numbers given are for J. & P. Coats craft yarn Art. E48.

COLOR KEY
STUDY TIME

Plastic Canvas Yarn	Yards
■ Black #00	1
□ Beige #40	12
□ White #41	8
Turquoise #54	2
■ Watermelon #55	½
□ Yellow #57	1
Bright orange #58	2
Uncoded areas on bear are maple #13 Continental Stitches	12
Uncoded area above bear is white #41 Continental Stitches	
╱ Maple #13 Whipstitching	
● Black #00 French Knot	
Heavy (#32) Braid	
╱ Black #005HL Backstitch	4

Color numbers given are for Uniek Needloft plastic canvas yarn and Kreinik Heavy (#32) Braid.

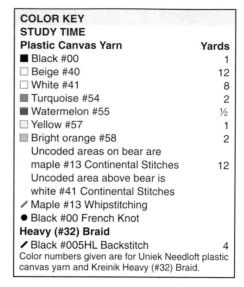

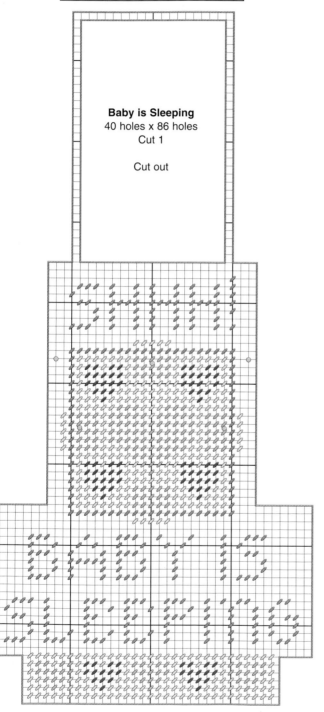

Baby is Sleeping
40 holes x 86 holes
Cut 1

Cut out

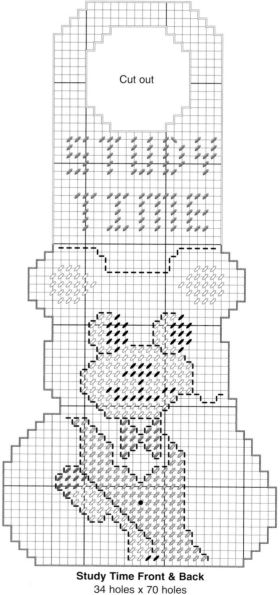

Cut out

Study Time Front & Back
34 holes x 70 holes
Cut 2, stitch 1

Fun-to-Stitch Photo Frames

Frame your youngster's photo in one of these three delightful children's photo frames.
They make a perfect decoration for any kid's room.

All Aboard Frame

Skill Level: Intermediate

Materials

- 1½ sheets Uniek Quick-Count 7-count clear plastic canvas
- 1 sheet light blue 7-count plastic canvas
- Uniek Needloft plastic canvas yarn as listed in color key
- DMC #3 pearl cotton as listed in color key
- 2 (10mm) round black cabochons
- Hot-glue gun

Project Notes

Instructions and yardage given are for sample project. Amount of yarn and number of train cars, small wheels and small wheel trims may change, depending on length of name used. One train car, one small wheel and one small wheel center are needed for each letter.

Each car uses 2 yards of either royal or yellow. Each small wheel uses approximately 12" black, and each small wheel center uses approximately 12" Christmas red. Each letter uses 18" of Christmas red.

Cutting & Stitching

1. Cut one frame back and two frame supports from light blue plastic canvas following graph (pages 128–130). Cut all remaining pieces from clear plastic canvas following graphs and project notes. Cut out photo opening on frame front only. Cut out slit for photo insertion on frame back only. Frame back and frame supports will remain unstitched.

2. Stitch and Overcast letters and small wheel trims with Christmas red following graphs. Stitch remaining pieces following graphs, reversing one cloud before stitching.

3. Work embroidery when background stitching is completed, wrapping pearl cotton around needle twice for French Knot nose and three times for French Knot eyes.

4. Overcast photo opening on frame front following graph. With sail blue, Whipstitch long straight edges of frame supports to frame back where indicated on graph. Whipstitch frame back to frame front with sail blue and Christmas green following graph.

5. Overcast bear ears and arm with maple, engine smoke with pewter and clouds with white and pewter following graphs. Overcast all remaining pieces with adjacent colors.

Assembly

1. Using photo as a guide through step 4, glue smoke to back of engine smokestack. Glue hat bill to hat and hat to bear's head. Glue head to front of train and hand to back of train. Glue ears to head front.

2. Center and glue heart to large wheel. Center and glue one small wheel trim to each small wheel. Glue left end of engine wheel bar to middle of one small wheel center; glue right end of bar to center of heart on large wheel. Glue wheels to engine, making sure bottom edges of wheels are even with bottom edge of cowcatcher.

3. Making sure bottom edges of train cars are even and alternating car colors, glue tongue of each car behind car to the left. Glue small wheels to bottom right edge of each car, making sure bottom edges of wheels are even. Glue one letter to each car, spelling name desired.

4. Glue tongue of first car to back of engine, making sure bottom edges are even. Glue entire train to frame front, making sure bottom edges are even.

—Design by Vicki Blizzard

All-Star Frame

Skill Level: Beginner

Materials

- 2 large sheets Darice Ultra Stiff 7-count plastic canvas
- ¼ sheet regular 7-count plastic canvas
- 3" 7-count plastic canvas Crafty Circle by Darice
- Uniek Needloft plastic canvas yarn as listed in color key
- Hot-glue gun

Instructions

1. Cut frame front and back from stiff plastic canvas; cut bat from regular plastic canvas according to graphs (pages 130 and 131). Cut out opening on frame front only. Cut outer row of holes from 3" circle according to graph. Frame back will remain unstitched.

2. Stitch pieces following graphs. Continental Stitch baseball with white, working seam stitches with Christmas red Straight Stitches when Continental Stitching is completed. For seam, thread Christmas red yarn under each Straight Stitch, pulling all the way through.

3. Overcast inside edges and top edge of frame front with orange, bat edges with camel and baseball edges with white. Whipstitch frame front to frame back around side and bottom edges with orange.

4. Glue baseball to upper left corner of frame front and bat to lower right corner. Hang as desired.

—Design by Marianne Telesca

Baby's First Photo Frame

Skill Level: Beginner

Materials

- 2 large sheets Darice Ultra Stiff 7-count plastic canvas
- ½ sheet regular 7-count plastic canvas
- Uniek Needloft plastic canvas yarn as listed in color key
- Hot-glue gun

Instructions

1. Cut frame front and back from stiff plastic canvas; cut blocks and rattle from regular plastic canvas according to graphs (page 132). Cut out opening on frame front only. Frame back will remain unstitched.

2. Stitch pieces following graphs. Continental Stitch blocks with white. Overcast inside edges and top edge of frame front with white, rattle edges with lemon and block edges with white. Work Backstitches on blocks when background stitching and Overcasting are completed.

3. Whipstitch frame front to frame back around side and bottom edges with white.

4. Glue rattle to upper left corner of frame front and blocks to lower right corner. Hang as desired.

—Design by Marianne Telesca

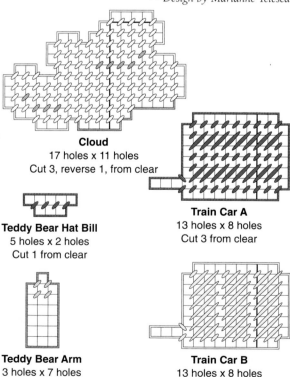

Cloud
17 holes x 11 holes
Cut 3, reverse 1, from clear

Teddy Bear Hat Bill
5 holes x 2 holes
Cut 1 from clear

Train Car A
13 holes x 8 holes
Cut 3 from clear

Teddy Bear Arm
3 holes x 7 holes
Cut 1 from clear

Train Car B
13 holes x 8 holes
Cut 2 from clear

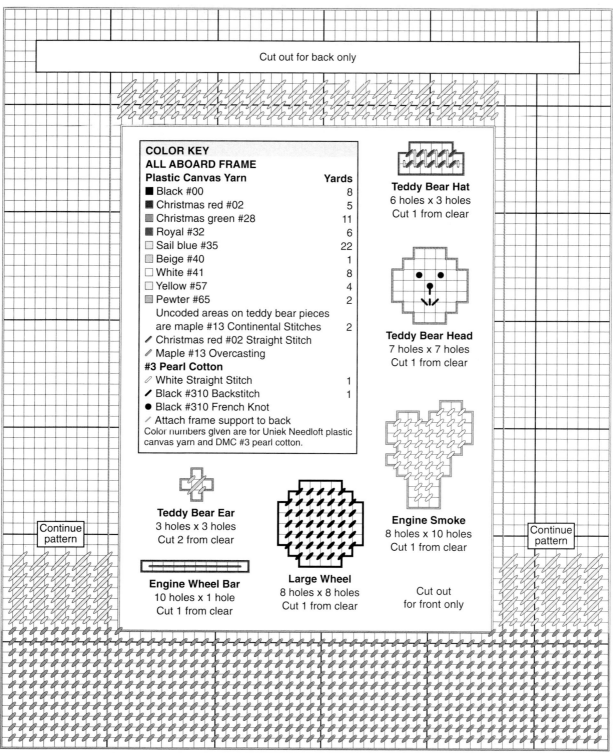

Cut out for back only

COLOR KEY
ALL ABOARD FRAME

Plastic Canvas Yarn	Yards
■ Black #00	8
■ Christmas red #02	5
■ Christmas green #28	11
■ Royal #32	6
□ Sail blue #35	22
■ Beige #40	1
□ White #41	8
□ Yellow #57	4
■ Pewter #65	2
Uncoded areas on teddy bear pieces are maple #13 Continental Stitches	2
✎ Christmas red #02 Straight Stitch	
✎ Maple #13 Overcasting	

#3 Pearl Cotton

✎ White Straight Stitch	1
✎ Black #310 Backstitch	1
● Black #310 French Knot	
✎ Attach frame support to back	

Color numbers given are for Uniek Needloft plastic canvas yarn and DMC #3 pearl cotton.

Teddy Bear Hat
6 holes x 3 holes
Cut 1 from clear

Teddy Bear Head
7 holes x 7 holes
Cut 1 from clear

Engine Smoke
8 holes x 10 holes
Cut 1 from clear

Teddy Bear Ear
3 holes x 3 holes
Cut 2 from clear

Engine Wheel Bar
10 holes x 1 hole
Cut 1 from clear

Large Wheel
8 holes x 8 holes
Cut 1 from clear

Cut out
for front only

Continue pattern

Continue pattern

All Aboard Frame Front & Back
57 holes x 69 holes
Cut 1 from clear for front
Stitch as graphed
Cut 1 from light blue for back
Do not stitch

Small Wheel
5 holes x 5 holes
Cut 6 from clear

Small Wheel Trim
3 holes x 3 holes
Cut 6 from clear

Large Wheel Heart
5 holes x 5 holes
Cut 1 from clear

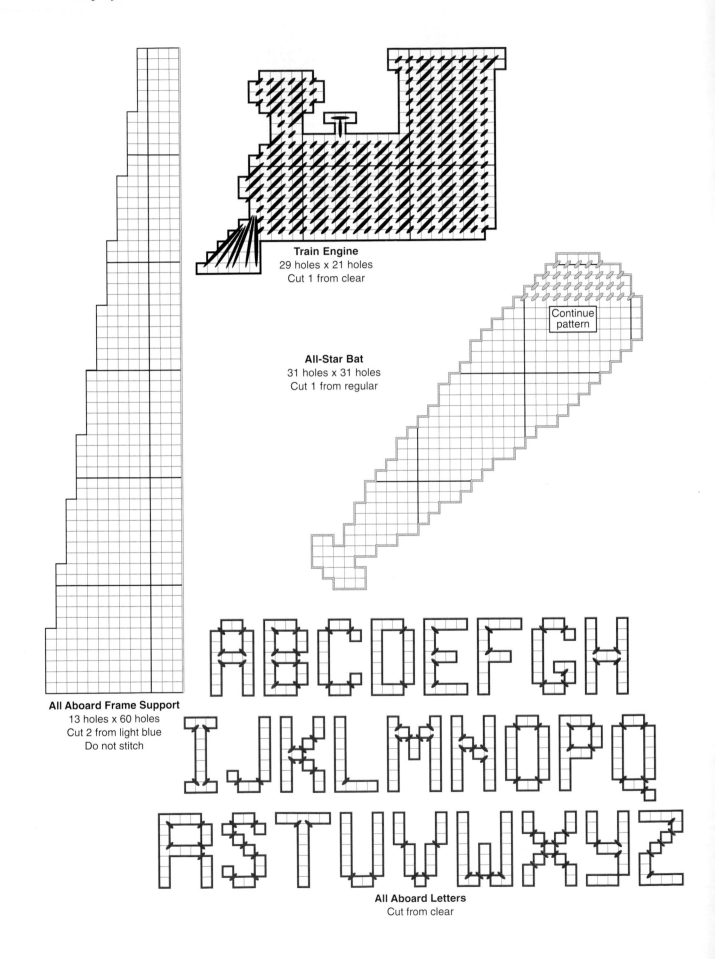

Train Engine
29 holes x 21 holes
Cut 1 from clear

All-Star Bat
31 holes x 31 holes
Cut 1 from regular

Continue
pattern

All Aboard Frame Support
13 holes x 60 holes
Cut 2 from light blue
Do not stitch

All Aboard Letters
Cut from clear

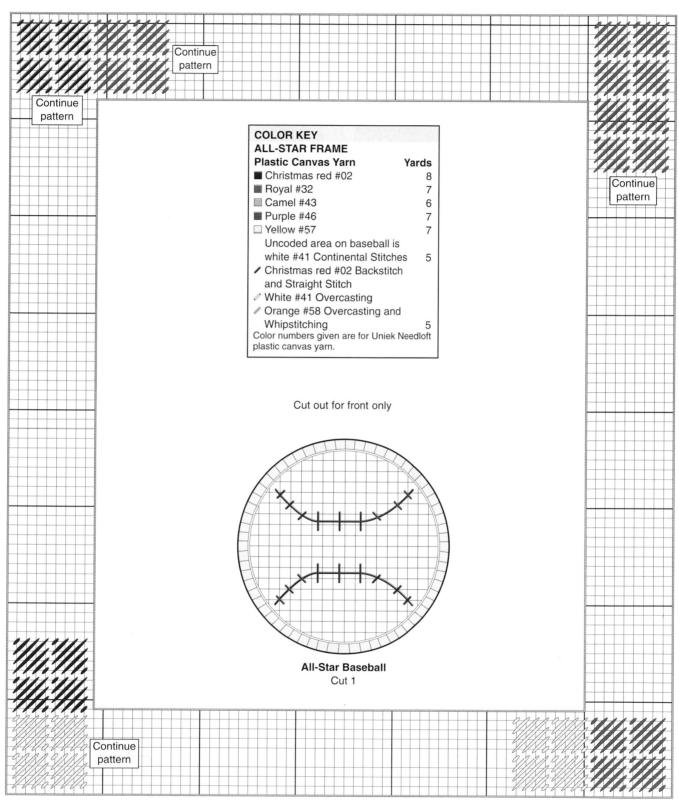

Continue pattern

Continue pattern

Continue pattern

Continue pattern

COLOR KEY
ALL-STAR FRAME

Plastic Canvas Yarn	Yards
■ Christmas red #02	8
■ Royal #32	7
▨ Camel #43	6
■ Purple #46	7
☐ Yellow #57	7
Uncoded area on baseball is white #41 Continental Stitches	5
✎ Christmas red #02 Backstitch and Straight Stitch	
✐ White #41 Overcasting	
✐ Orange #58 Overcasting and Whipstitching	5

Color numbers given are for Uniek Needloft plastic canvas yarn.

Cut out for front only

All-Star Baseball
Cut 1

All-Star Frame Front & Back
69 holes x 81 holes
Cut 2 from stiff

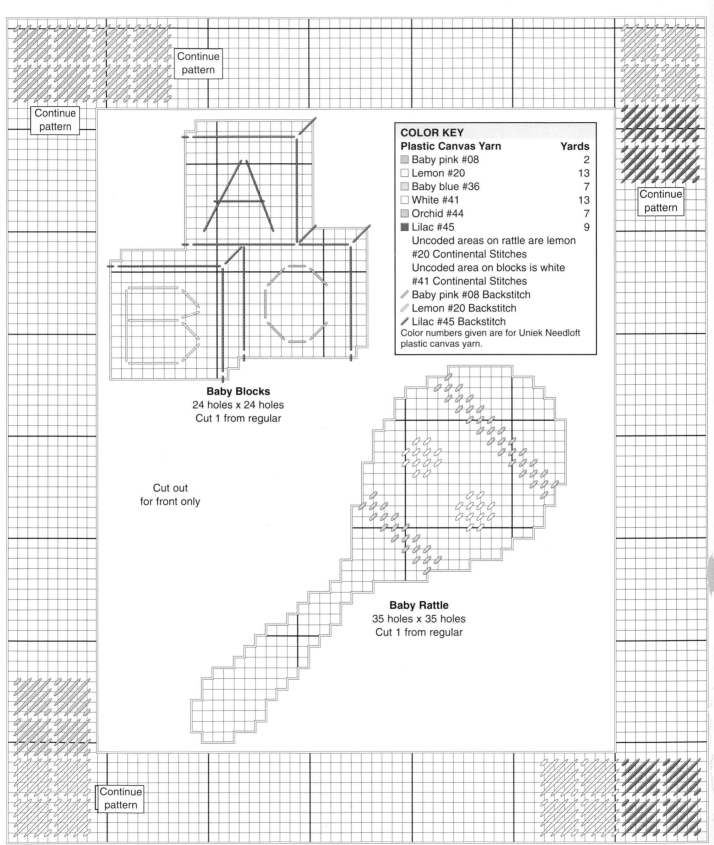

Continue pattern

Continue pattern

Continue pattern

COLOR KEY

Plastic Canvas Yarn	Yards
■ Baby pink #08	2
□ Lemon #20	13
■ Baby blue #36	7
□ White #41	13
▨ Orchid #44	7
■ Lilac #45	9

Uncoded areas on rattle are lemon #20 Continental Stitches
Uncoded area on blocks is white #41 Continental Stitches
✎ Baby pink #08 Backstitch
✎ Lemon #20 Backstitch
✎ Lilac #45 Backstitch

Color numbers given are for Uniek Needloft plastic canvas yarn.

Baby Blocks
24 holes x 24 holes
Cut 1 from regular

Cut out
for front only

Baby Rattle
35 holes x 35 holes
Cut 1 from regular

Continue pattern

Continue pattern

Baby First Photo Frame Front & Back
69 holes x 81 holes
Cut 2 from stiff

green ribbon, stitching two or three times at corners as necessary to cover.

3. Fold grosgrain ribbon in half over key chain; glue short ends together. Center ribbon on top backside of stitched piece so that folded end is ½" above top edge. Glue synthetic suede or felt over ribbon to backside of piece, trimming as needed. Allow to dry thoroughly.

—Design by Judi Kauffman

COLOR KEY	
6-Strand Embroidery Floss	**Yards**
☐ Ecru	3
■ Very dark dusty rose #3350	3
Uncoded areas are Christmas green #699 Continental Stitches	6
Medium (#16) Braid	
▨ Pearl #032	1
☐ Confetti fuchsia #042	1
¹⁄₁₆ " Ribbon	
╱ Green #008 Overcasting	1

Color numbers given are for DMC 6-strand embroidery floss, Kreinik Medium (#16) Braid and ¹⁄₁₆ " Ribbon.

Ho-Ho-Ho Key Chain

Stitch this easy-to-make project as a stocking stuffer. Imagine the recipient's delight if the key chain included keys to a brand-new car!

Skill Level: Beginner

Materials

- Small amount 14-count plastic canvas
- DMC 6-strand embroidery floss as listed in color key
- Kreinik Medium (#16) Braid as listed in color key
- Kreinik ¹⁄₁₆" Ribbon as listed in color key
- Tapestry needle
- 2½" ⅞"-wide raspberry grosgrain ribbon
- 1¼"-diameter silver split key ring
- 1¾" x 3" piece green or raspberry synthetic suede or felt
- Tacky glue

Instructions

1. Cut plastic canvas according to graph.

2. Stitch piece following graph. Overcast with

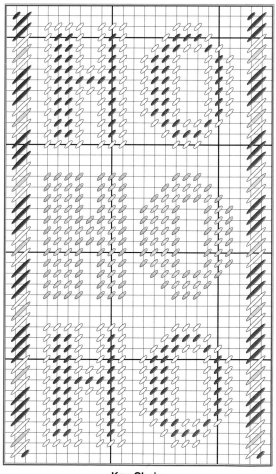

Key Chain
25 holes x 43 holes
Cut 1

Jingle Bell Ornaments

Complete your tree trims with Santa and Frosty! With their cheery faces, rosy cheeks and golden jingle bells, they'll make a delightful addition to your holiday decor!

Skill Level: Beginner

Materials

- 1 sheet 7-count plastic canvas
- Spinrite plastic canvas yarn as listed in color key
- DMC #3 pearl cotton as listed in color key
- Kreinik Fine (#8) Braid: 1 yard gold #002
- #16 tapestry needle
- 2 (7mm) ruby frosted cabochons from The Beadery
- 4 (6mm) black round cabochons from The Beadery
- 5 (4mm) black round cabochons from The Beadery
- 10.5mm x 10mm ruby heart cabochon from The Beadery
- 3 (4mm) ruby round faceted stones from The Beadery
- 4 (19mm x 10.5mm) emerald faceted holly leaves from The Beadery
- 2 (½") gold jingle bells
- Small frosted crystal heart charm
- 6" ⅛"-wide white satin ribbon

Instructions

1. Cut plastic canvas according to graphs (page 139).

2. Stitch pieces following graphs, reversing snowman back and Santa back before stitching. Work head and beard on Santa back and head on snowman back with white Continental Stitches only.

Work embroidery on fronts when background stitching is completed.

3. Overcast Santa hat tip with wine and Santa mustache with white. Whipstitch wrong sides of Santa front and back together along inside and outside edges, using wine for hat and white for hat cuff, face and beard. With wrong side of hat tip on right side of hat, Whipstitch top edges of both pieces together with wine.

4. Whipstitch wrong sides of snowman front and back together along inside and outside edges, using royal for hat, white for face and wine for scarf.

5. Using photo as a guide through step 9, glue mustache to Santa. For Santa and snowman, glue on 6mm black cabochons for eyes and 7mm frosted ruby cabochons for noses. Glue 4mm black cabochons to snowman for mouth.

6. Glue three 4mm ruby faceted stones and two emerald leaves to right side of Santa's hat. Glue ruby heart and two emerald leaves to left side of snowman's hat.

7. With fine gold braid, attach heart charm to bottom hole of hat tip. Tie a small bow with white ribbon and glue to hat tip.

8. Tie a short length of gold braid to each bell, then thread braid from front to back on ornaments where indicated on graphs, tying in back and trimming as needed.

9. For hanger, cut one 10" length of gold braid for each ornament. Attach hangers to tops of ornaments where indicated on graphs. Tie ends in a knot and trim.

—Designs by Vicki Blizzard

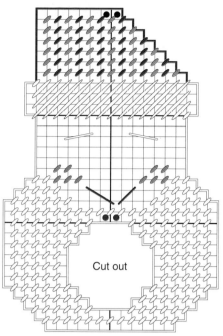

Santa Ornament Front & Back
20 holes x 30 holes
Cut 2, reverse 1

COLOR KEY
SNOWMAN

Plastic Canvas Yarn	Yards
■ Pale pink #0003	½
■ Wine #0011	2
■ Scarlet #0022	2
■ Royal #0026	4
Uncoded areas are white #0001 Continental Stitches	5

#3 Pearl Cotton
✔ Black #310 Backstitch	¼
● Attach bell	
● Attach hanger	

Color numbers given are for Spinrite plastic canvas yarn and DMC #3 pearl cotton.

COLOR KEY
SANTA

Plastic Canvas Yarn	Yards
☐ White #0001	10
■ Cherry blossom #0010	½
■ Wine #0011	3
■ Scarlet #0022	2
Uncoded areas are pale pink #0003 Continental Stitches	1
✎ White #0001 Straight Stitch	

#3 Pearl Cotton
✔ Christmas red #321 Backstitch	¼
● Attach bell	
● Attach hanger	

Color numbers given are for Spinrite plastic canvas yarn and DMC #3 pearl cotton.

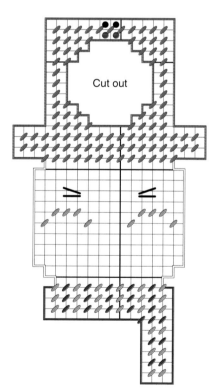

Snowman Ornament Front & Back
18 holes x 34 holes
Cut 2, reverse 1

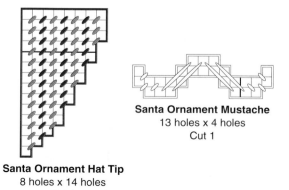

Santa Ornament Hat Tip
8 holes x 14 holes
Cut 1

Santa Ornament Mustache
13 holes x 4 holes
Cut 1

Instructions

1. Cut plastic canvas according to graphs (below and page 141).

2. Stitch pieces following graphs. Work embroidery over completed background stitching.

3. Overcast wreath frame front and back with Christmas green, star frame front and back and inside edges of poinsettia frame front with gold craft cord and remaining edges of poinsettia frame front and back with red.

4. Center and glue one magnetic strip to wrong side of each frame back. Center photo in photo opening, then place frame fronts on corresponding frame backs so that frame front points are between frame back points. Push front points back, locking them behind back points.

—Designs by Angie Arickx

Wreath Frame Back
19 holes x 19 holes
Cut 1

Holiday Frames

Display your most precious treasures in these quick and easy-to-stitch magnets!

Skill Level: Beginner

Materials

- 1 sheet 7-count plastic canvas
- Uniek Needloft plastic canvas yarn as listed in color key
- Uniek Needloft metallic craft cord as listed in color key
- #16 tapestry needle
- 3 (1") magnetic strips
- Hot-glue gun

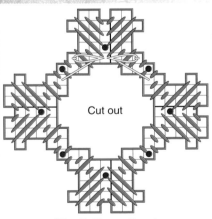

Wreath Frame Front
19 holes x 19 holes
Cut 1

COLOR KEY

Plastic Canvas Yarn	Yards
■ Christmas red #02	6
▨ Gold #17	5
▨ Christmas green #28	7
✎ Red #01 Overcasting	3
● Christmas red #02 French Knot	

Metallic Craft Cord

✎ Gold #01 Straight Stitch and Overcasting	4
○ Gold #01 French Knot	
✐ Gold #01 Lazy Daisy	

Color numbers given are for Uniek Needloft plastic canvas yarn and craft cord.

Poinsettia Frame Front
23 holes x 23 holes
Cut 1

Poinsettia Frame Back
27 holes x 27 holes
Cut 1

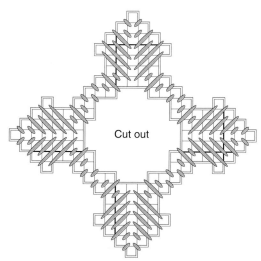

Star Frame Front
23 holes x 23 holes
Cut 1

Star Frame Back
23 holes x 23 holes
Cut 1

Fun With Rudolph

What child doesn't dream of meeting Rudolph the Red-Nosed Reindeer? Delight your little ones with Rudolph pins and lollipop ornaments!

Skill Level: Beginner

Materials
Each Project
- ⅓ sheet 7-count plastic canvas
- Plastic canvas yarn as listed in color key
- #16 tapestry needle
- ½" red pompon
- 6mm gold jingle bell
- Hot-glue gun

Pin
- 1½" pin back
- Floral picks:
  1 with holly leaves and berries
  1 with evergreen
- Sewing needle and tan sewing thread

Lollipop Ornament
- 8" ⅛"-wide red satin ribbon
- Round lollipop
- Sewing needle and green sewing thread

Instructions

1. Cut plastic canvas according to graphs (below and page 143).

2. Stitch ornament pieces following graphs, working Slanting Gobelin Stitches on face and Continental Stitches first. Work dark brown Backstitches for mouth. Complete stitching, bending plastic canvas back and overlapping two holes where indicated.

3. Overcast bow tie with green. Overcast antlers on ornament with dark brown and remaining edges with tan.

4. Using photo as a guide through step 5, with sewing needle and green thread, sew bow tie below mouth where indicated on graph. Sew one jingle bell to Rudolph below bow tie.

5. Thread red satin ribbon from front to back where indicated on graph; tie ends in a knot to form a loop for hanging. Glue one red pompon to face over red stitches. Insert lollipop in ornament.

6. Stitch pin following graph. Overcast antlers with dark brown and remaining edges with tan. Work Backstitches when background stitching and Overcasting are completed.

7. Using photo as a guide through step 8, with sewing needle and tan thread, sew remaining jingle bell to center bottom of face. Glue remaining pompon to face over red stitches.

8. Cut two evergreen leaves from pick and glue to bottom backside of face. Cut one holly leaf and one berry from pick and glue below one antler. Glue pin back to backside of stitched piece.

—*Designs by Kristine Loffredo*

COLOR KEY	
ORNAMENT	
Plastic Canvas Yarn	**Yards**
☐ Tan	4
▨ Dark brown	2
▩ Green	1½
▨ Pink	½
■ Red	½
■ Black	½
☐ White	½
╱ Dark brown Backstitch	
● Attach bow tie	
● Attach red satin ribbon	

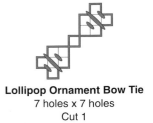

Lollipop Ornament Bow Tie
7 holes x 7 holes
Cut 1

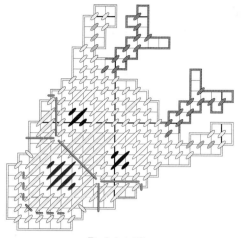

Rudolph Pin
21 holes x 21 holes
Cut 1

COLOR KEY
PIN

Plastic Canvas Yarn	Yards
☐ Tan	3½
▨ Dark brown	2
▨ Pink	½
■ Red	½
■ Black	½
☐ White	½
╱ Green Backstitch	½
╱ Dark brown Backstitch	

Let it Snow! Pin

Welcome winter with this dapper snowman pin! Tiny French knots look like glistening snowflakes against a deep blue sky.

Skill Level: Intermediate

Materials
- Small amount 14-count plastic canvas
- DMC 6-strand embroidery floss as listed in color key
- Kreinik Fine (#8) Braid as listed in color key
- #26 tapestry needle
- 3 (10mm) gold jump rings
- 1¼" gold pin back
- Glue gun

Instructions
1. Cut one pin and three snowflakes from plastic canvas according to graphs (page 151).

2. Using 3 strands throughout when working with floss, Cross Stitch pin and snowflakes following graphs. Work embroidery when background stitching is completed, replacing pearl Backstitches and French Knots on one snowflake with pale yellow and on remaining snowflake with pale green.

3. Overcast snowflakes with navy floss and pin with navy floss and pearl braid following graphs.

4. Attach one jump ring to center top hole of each snowflake, then attach jump rings to pin where indicated on graph, matching color of snowflake under same color snowman. Glue pin back to wrong side of pin.

—Design by Vicki Blizzard

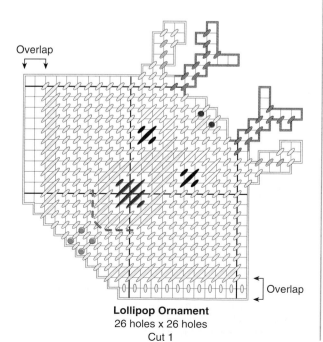

Overlap

Overlap

Lollipop Ornament
26 holes x 26 holes
Cut 1

Holly Wreaths Garland

Hang this elegant garland over a doorway or above the mantel for a sophisticated plastic canvas decoration.

Skill Level: Beginner

Materials

- 1 sheet 7-count plastic canvas
- 6 (6") radial circles
- Red Heart Classic worsted weight yarn Art. E267 as listed in color key
- #16 tapestry needle
- ⅜"-wide ribbon:
    9 yards red picot-edge satin
    9 yards gold metallic
- 54 (18mm) gold star flower beads by The Beadery
- 54 (4mm) round ruby cabochons by The Beadery
- 6" piece cardboard
- Hot-glue gun

Project Note

Instructions and amounts given are for six wreaths with an 18" garland between each wreath. Ten holly leaves are needed for each wreath and 10 for each 18" strand of garland. Nine gold star flower beads, nine round ruby cabochons and 54" each of red and gold ribbon are used for each wreath.

Instructions

1. Cut leaves from plastic canvas and centers from plastic canvas circles according to graphs (right and page 146).

2. Using paddy green through step 3, stitch leaves and wreaths following graphs. Work Straight Stitches on leaves when background stitching is completed. Overcast inside and outside edges of circles.

3. To form one 18" strand of garland, join 10 leaves together at tips while Overcasting. Repeat four more times to make a total of five strands. Overcast remaining leaves.

4. Using photo as a guide, glue 10 holly leaves to wrong side of each stitched circle, overlapping ends slightly and leaving the space open between dots at bottom of wreaths for bows.

5. Glue or stitch garland ends to bottoms of wreaths where indicated on graph. Glue red cabochons to centers of gold flower beads. Using photo as a guide, glue flower beads to tips of leaves around sides and tops of wreaths.

6. For each bow, wrap 42" of gold and red ribbon around a 6" piece of cardboard. Slide loops off cardboard and tie in center with one 12" length of gold and red ribbon held together. Trim ends as desired. Glue one bow to bottom center of each wreath.

7. Hang as desired.

—Design by Vicki Blizzard

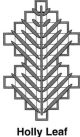

Holly Leaf
7 holes x 11 holes
Cut 110

COLOR KEY

Worsted Weight Yarn	Yards
■ Paddy green #686	150
╱ Paddy green #686 Straight Stitch	
● Attach garland	

Color numbers given are for Red Heart Classic worsted weight yarn Art. E267.

Fancy Wreaths Basket

Tuck a special gift into this pretty basket designed with ice-crystal patterned sides and adorned with elegant wreaths!

Skill Level: Advanced

Materials

- 1½ sheets 10-count plastic canvas
- Anchor #3 pearl cotton as listed in color key

Instructions

1. Cut plastic canvas according to graphs (right and page 146). Cut one 49-hole x 49-hole piece for basket bottom. Basket bottom will remain unstitched.

2. Stitch pieces following graphs, reversing two tails before stitching. Work French Knots on wreath handles when background stitching is completed.

3. Overcast inner and outer edges of handles with very dark grass green. Overcast bows and tails with crimson red. Using white throughout, Overcast top edges of basket sides. Whipstitch sides together, then Whipstitch sides to bottom.

4. Use photo as a guide throughout assembly. Using crimson red throughout, for each bow, tack tops of two tails together so that inside edges are facing center. Fold bow ends to backside of bow where indicated on graph with blue line; tack in place. Attach tails to center backside of bows.

5. Attach bows to bottom section of wreath handles. With white, attach wreath handles to opposite sides of basket so that bottom edge of wreath opening is even with center top edge of basket side.

—Design by Judi Kauffman

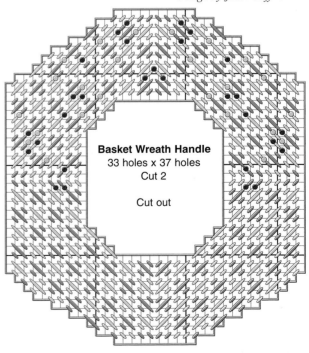

Basket Wreath Handle
33 holes x 37 holes
Cut 2

Cut out

Basket Side
49 holes x 37 holes
Cut 4

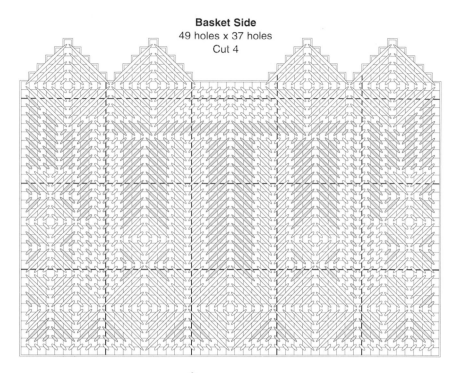

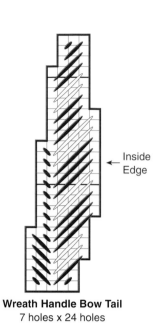

→ Inside
Edge

Wreath Handle Bow Tail
7 holes x 24 holes
Cut 4, reverse 2

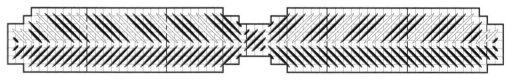

Wreath Handle Bow
62 holes x 8 holes
Cut 2

Holly Wreaths Garland

Continued from page 144

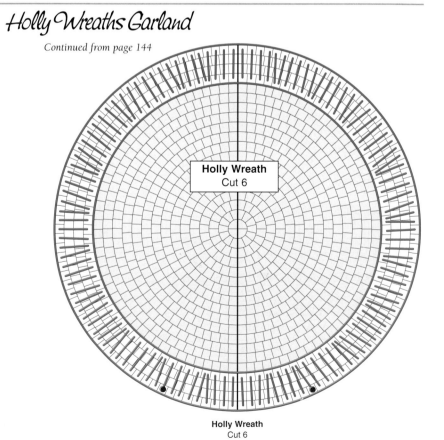

Holly Wreath
Cut 6

Holly Wreath
Cut 6

COLOR KEY
#3 Pearl Cotton

		Yards
☐	White #1	85
☐	Crimson red #46	18
☐	Light cobalt blue #128	30
☐	Medium grass green #243	11
☐	Very dark grass green #246	15
●	Crimson red #46 French Knot	
○	Light grass green #240 French Knot	4

Color numbers given are for Anchor #3 pearl cotton.

Li'l Christmas Angels

Add a touch of heavenly charm to your home this Christmas! Each of these delightful angels can decorate a wall or door with endearing sweetness.

Country Angel

Skill Level: Intermediate

Materials

- ½ sheet 7-count plastic canvas
- J. & P. Coats plastic canvas yarn as listed in color key
- Anchor 6-strand embroidery floss as listed in color key
- 18" ⅛"-wide yellow-gold satin ribbon
- 27" 22-gauge steel wire
- Pencil
- Pliers
- Wire cutters

Instructions

1. Cut plastic canvas according to graphs (page 148).

2. Stitch pieces following graphs. Overcast hearts and angel with adjacent colors. Work Backstitches with 6 strands floss when background stitching and Overcasting are completed.

3. Cut a 9" length of yellow-gold ribbon. Using photo as a guide through step 8, on one heart, thread ribbon from back to front through one of the holes indicated on heart graph with blue dot, then from front to back through remaining hole with blue dot.

4. Repeat with two more hearts, centering all three hearts on ribbon, allowing slightly less than ¼" between hearts. Thread ribbon ends through holes indicated on angel graph from front to back, centering hearts between angel's hands. Knot ribbon ends on backside, trimming excess.

5. Insert one end of wire through hole indicated on wing on right side. Twist 1" of end around wire to secure. Make a few coils by wrapping wire around pencil.

6. On opposite end, thread on remaining two hearts from back to front through one hole indicated with blue dot on heart, then from front to back through remaining hole with blue dot.

7. Insert wire end through hole indicated on wing on left side, wrapping 1" of end around wire to secure. Coil wire between this end and heart two or three times around pencil. Make a loop for hanging by twisting wire in center.

8. Tie remaining ribbon in a bow between hearts.

—Design by Nancy Marshall

Flying Angel

Skill Level: Beginner

Materials

- ½ sheet 7-count plastic canvas
- Uniek Needloft plastic canvas yarn as listed in color key
- DMC #3 pearl cotton as listed in color key
- 1 yard ⅝"-wide gold wire-edged ribbon

Instructions

1. Cut plastic canvas according to graph (page 149).

2. Stitch piece following graph. Work embroidery when background stitching is completed. Overcast inside edges with yellow and outside edges with denim.

3. Thread ribbon ends from back to front through holes at top. Tie ends in a bow to form a loop for hanging.

—*Design by Michele Wilcox*

COLOR KEY	
COUNTRY ANGEL	
Plastic Canvas Yarn	**Yards**
☐ Natural #111	9
☐ Sea coral #246	2
▨ Medium brown #337	2
▨ Honey gold #645	3
▨ Paddy green #686	3
▨ Lily pink #719	1
■ Windsor blue #808	1
■ Cardinal #917	5
Uncoded area is tan #334	
Continental Stitches	3
6-Strand Embroidery Floss	
✒ Deep red #22 Backstitch	¼
✒ Black #403 Backstitch	¼
⬤ Attach yellow gold ribbon	
● Attach wire	
Color numbers given are for J. & P. Coats plastic canvas yarn and Anchor 6-strand embroidery floss.	

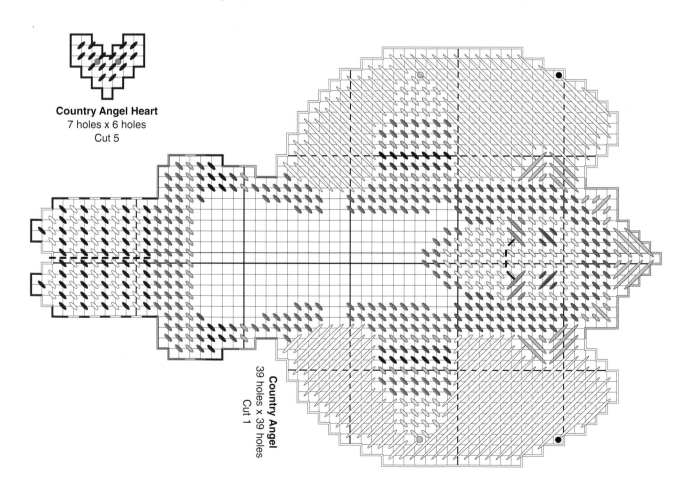

Country Angel Heart
7 holes x 6 holes
Cut 5

Country Angel
39 holes x 39 holes
Cut 1

COLOR KEY
FLYING ANGEL

Plastic Canvas Yarn	Yards
■ Red #01	1
■ Gold #17	1
■ Denim #33	18
□ Cerulean #34	1
□ White #41	2
□ Flesh tone #56	2
Uncoded area is yellow #57 Continental Stitches	24
╱ Yellow #57 Overcasting	

#3 Pearl Cotton

╱ Black #310 Straight Stitch	⅙
╱ Bright Christmas red #666 Backstitch	3
● Bright Christmas red #666 French Knot	
● Dark peacock blue #806 French Knot	⅙
● Copper #919 French Knot	2

Color numbers given are for Uniek Needloft plastic canvas yarn and DMC #3 pearl cottton.

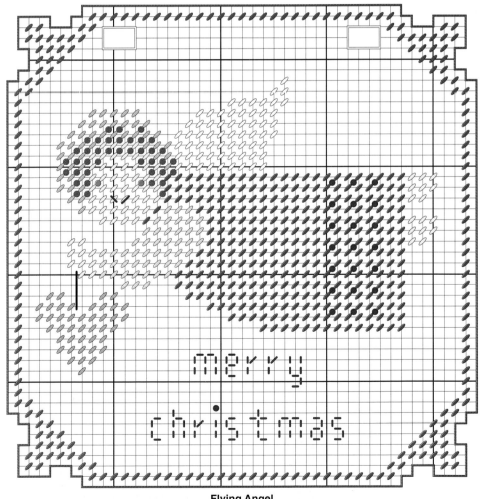

Flying Angel
44 holes x 45 holes
Cut 1

Mini Stockings

These little stockings are just the right size for filling with small candies and gifts, or even for hanging on the tree!

Skill Level: Beginner

Materials

- 1 sheet 7-count plastic canvas
- Uniek Needloft plastic canvas yarn as listed in color key
- DMC #3 pearl cotton as listed in color key
- ½ yard each ¼"-wide green and red satin ribbon

Instructions

1. Cut plastic canvas according to graphs (page 151).

2. Stitch stocking fronts following graphs; reverse stocking backs before stitching. Work Backstitches when background stitching is completed.

3. Overcast top edges of each stocking piece with white. Whipstitch wrong sides of Joy Stocking together with red around side and bottom edges following graphs. Whipstitch wrong sides of Ho Ho

Ho Stocking together around sides and bottom with Christmas green.

4. Thread red satin ribbon through top back seam of Joy Stocking and green satin ribbon through top back seam of Ho Ho Ho Stocking. Tie ends in bows to form loops for hanging.

—Designs by Michele Wilcox

COLOR KEY	
Plastic Canvas Yarn	**Yards**
■ Red #01	16
▨ Christmas green #28	18
☐ White #41	26
Uncoded areas are white #41 Continental Stitches	
#3 Pearl Cotton	
⁄ Bright Christmas red #666 Backstitch	1
⁄ Kelly green #701 Backstitch	2
◉ Bright Christmas red #666 French Knot	
Color numbers given are for Uniek Needloft plastic canvas yarn and DMC #3 pearl cotton.	

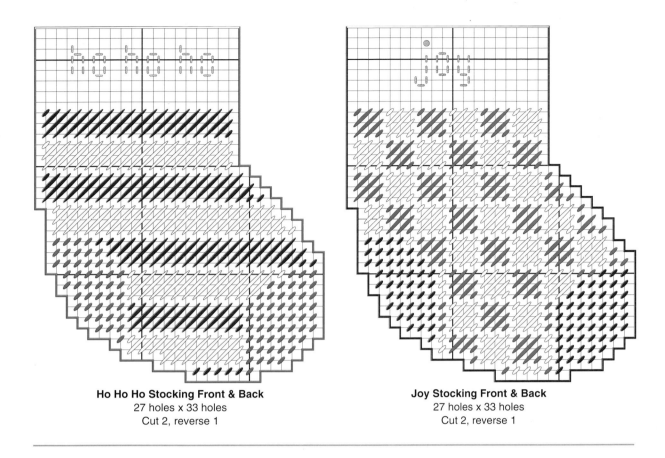

Ho Ho Ho Stocking Front & Back
27 holes x 33 holes
Cut 2, reverse 1

Joy Stocking Front & Back
27 holes x 33 holes
Cut 2, reverse 1

Let it Snow! Pin

Continued from page 143

COLOR KEY
6-Strand Embroidery Floss	Yards
■ Bright Christmas red #666	⅓
■ Bright Christmas green #700	⅓
□ Deep canary #725	⅓
Uncoded areas are navy blue #336 Cross Stitches	3
⁄ Navy blue #336 Overcasting	
⁄ Dark burnt orange #608 Straight Stitch	⅓
⁄ Bright Christmas red #666 Backstitch	
⁄ Bright Christmas green #700 Backstitch	
⁄ Deep canary #725 Backstitch	
Fine (#8) Braid	
□ Pearl #032	3
▨ Pale yellow #191	1½
□ Pale green #198	1½
⁄ Black #005 Backstitch	1
⁄ Pearl #032 Backstitch	
⁄ Aztec gold #202HL Backstitch	1
● Black #005 French Knot	
○ Pearl #032 French Knot	
◉ Attach jump ring	

Color numbers given are for DMC 6-strand embroidery floss and Kreinik Fine (#8) Braid.

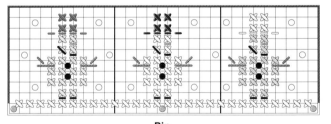

Pin
29 holes x 10 holes
Cut 1

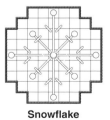

Snowflake
9 holes x 9 holes
Cut 3
Stitch 1 as graphed
Stitch 1 replacing pearl with pale yellow
Stitch 1 replacing pearl with pale green

Santa Window Ornament

Add a touch of country charm to your home with this cute Santa window ornament.

Skill Level: Beginner

Materials

- ½ sheet 7-count plastic canvas
- Uniek Needloft plastic canvas yarn as listed in color key
- #3 pearl cotton as listed in color key
- 30" ¼"-wide red satin ribbon

Instructions

1. Cut plastic canvas according to graph.

2. Continental Stitch piece following graph. Work black pearl cotton French Knots when background stitching is completed. Overcast with adjacent colors.

3. Attach red satin ribbon with a Lark's Head Knot (Fig. 1) around center top of heart. Tie ends in a bow to form a loop for hanging; trim as desired.

—*Design by Michele Wilcox*

COLOR KEY

Plastic Canvas Yarn	Yards
■ Red #01	4
▨ Christmas green #28	8
☐ White #41	1
▧ Flesh tone #56	1
#3 Pearl Cotton	
● Black French Knot	¼

Color numbers given are for Uniek Needloft plastic canvas yarn.

Fig. 1
Lark's Head Knot

Santa Window Ornament
37 holes x 31 holes
Cut 1

Holiday Gift Bag

Looking for a special gift to take to this year's Christmas dinner hostess?
Place a gift inside this lovely bag for two presents in one!

Skill Level: Beginner

Materials

- 2½ sheets 7-count plastic canvas
- 2 (5") plastic canvas stars by Uniek
- Anchor #3 pearl cotton as listed in color key
- 4mm metallic GlissenGloss Braid Ribbon 4 by Madeira as listed in color key
- #16 tapestry needle
- Glue gun

Project Notes

Work with 2 strands pearl cotton and 1 strand braid ribbon throughout project.

Keep pearl cotton and braid ribbon smooth and flat by guiding between thumb and forefinger and by dropping needle occasionally to allow pearl cotton and braid ribbon to unwind.

Instructions

1. Cut plastic canvas according to graphs (page 154). Cut one 37-hole x 21-hole piece for bag bottom and two 1-hole x 76-hole pieces for bag handles. Bag bottom will remain unstitched.

2. Stitch pieces following graphs. Whipstitch slits in sides together with Christmas red, forming pleats.

3. Using a 1½-yard length of dark gold, thread braid ribbon through first hole of handle, leaving a 1" tail. Remove needle. Keeping braid ribbon smooth and flat, wrap ribbon over tail and around handle, overlapping edges enough to cover plastic canvas. Continue wrapping to opposite end of handle. Thread braid ribbon onto needle, go through last hole and weave tail under last few wraps. Repeat for remaining handle.

4. Using dark gold throughout, Overcast stars across outside row of holes. Overcast top edges of bag front, back and sides. Whipstitch front and back to sides, then Whipstitch front, back and sides to bottom.

5. Using photo as a guide through step 6, position stars on bag front and back. Attach each star at center with ultra dark pistachio green, stitching enough times to cover canvas. Tack four points of each star to bag with dark gold.

6. Position ends of one handle between star and unstitched portion of bag front; glue in place. Repeat with remaining handle, gluing to bag back.

—Design by Kathy Wirth

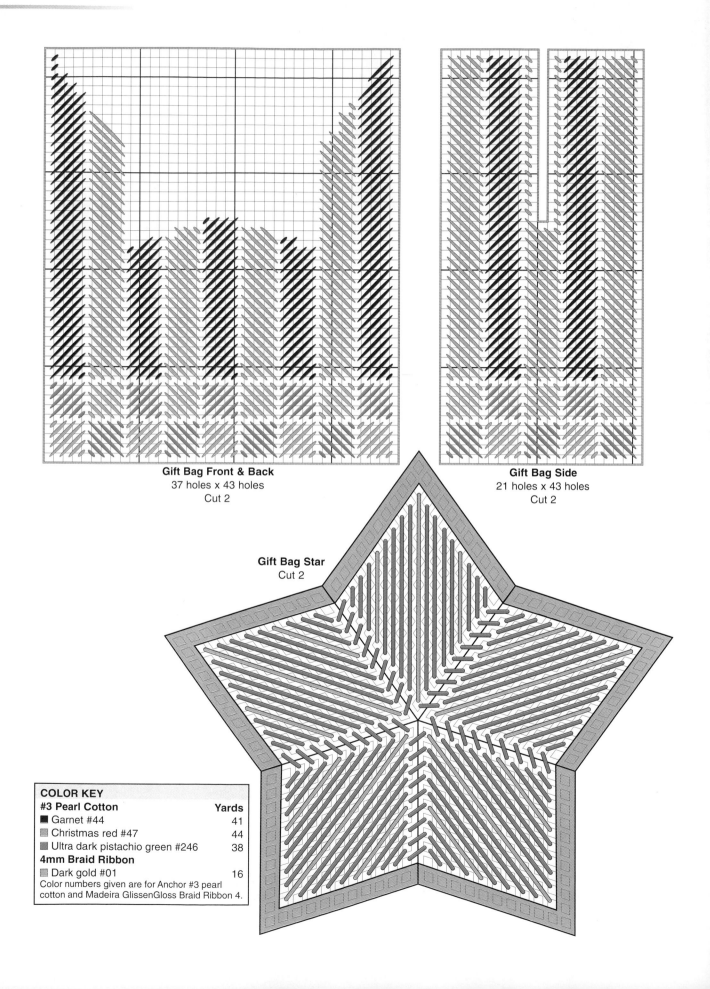

Gift Bag Front & Back
37 holes x 43 holes
Cut 2

Gift Bag Side
21 holes x 43 holes
Cut 2

Gift Bag Star
Cut 2

COLOR KEY

#3 Pearl Cotton	Yards
■ Garnet #44	41
▨ Christmas red #47	44
▨ Ultra dark pistachio green #246	38
4mm Braid Ribbon	
▨ Dark gold #01	16

Color numbers given are for Anchor #3 pearl
cotton and Madeira GlissenGloss Braid Ribbon 4.

Chubby Angel Trio

These darling musical angels are making a joyful noise!
Let them make a joyful decoration in your home this Christmas!

Skill Level: Intermediate

Materials

- ½ sheet 10-count plastic canvas
- DMC #3 pearl cotton as listed in color key
- DMC 6-strand embroidery floss as listed in color key
- Kreinik Fine (#8) Braid as listed in color key
- Kreinik Medium (#16) Braid as listed in color key
- #20 tapestry needle
- Kreinik ⅛" Ribbon: ½ yard gold #002
- 6 (5mm) round black cabochons by The Beadery
- 2 (⅜") gold jingle bells
- 7 (¼") gold jingle bells
- White mini-curl doll hair by One & Only Creations
- ½ yard white gold-edged pre-gathered lace
- 3 pairs white goose-feather angel wings
- ¼ yard green-and-gold print fabric
- ¼ yard red-and-gold print fabric
- ¼ yard navy-and-gold print fabric
- Sewing needle and matching sewing thread
- Polyester fiberfill
- Hot-glue gun

Heads & Halos

1. Cut two head pieces and one halo for each angel according to graphs (page 157).

2. Stitch head fronts following graphs. Stitch head backs, working necks in very light peach flesh Continental Stitches and heads in snow white Continental Stitches. Work embroidery on head fronts when background stitching is completed, wrapping pearl cotton around needle three times for French Knot noses.

3. With wrong sides facing, Whipstitch each head dart and each neck dart together with very light peach flesh. With wrong sides facing, Whipstitch head fronts to head backs with very light peach flesh and snow white following graphs, stuffing head firmly with fiberfill before closing.

4. Using photo as a guide through step 5, glue cabochons to head fronts for eyes. Glue hair to head following manufacturer's instructions.

5. Stitch and Overcast halos following graph. Glue to tops of heads.

Arms & Base

1. Cut four arms and one base for each angel according to graphs (page 157).

2. For bell angel, stitch four arms, reversing two, following graphs. For caroling angel, stitch four arms, reversing two, replacing Christmas red with ultra dark pistachio green. For tambourine angel, stitch four arms, reversing two, replacing Christmas red with navy blue.

3. With wrong sides together and matching edges, Whipstitch each angel's arms together with adjacent colors.

4. For bell angel, stitch base following graph, overlapping one hole before stitching. Overcast top and bottom edges with Christmas red. Repeat with remaining two bases, stitching caroling angel base with ultra dark pistachio green and tambourine angel base with navy blue.

Angel Accessories

1. Cut two carols book covers, two carols book pages, four bell handles and one tambourine according to graphs (page 157).

2. Continental Stitch pieces following graphs, overlapping one hole on tambourine before stitching. When background stitching is completed, work embroidery with gold fine braid on one book cover only; work Straight Stitches with black floss on both book pages.

3. Using dark mahogany throughout, Overcast top and bottom edges of tambourine. Whipstitch

wrong sides of two bell handles together. Repeat with remaining two bell handles.

4. Glue ¼" bells evenly spaced around outside of tambourine, leaving a space at seam for hand. Glue one ⅜" bell to one end of each bell handle.

5. With Christmas red and with wrong sides together, Whipstitch cover pieces together along one long edge from dot to dot; Overcast remaining edges.

6. With right sides together, Whipstitch one long edge of book pages together with snow white. Overcast remaining edges with gold medium braid. With wrong sides together, center and glue pages to cover.

Body & Angel Assembly

1. For angel bodies, from each piece of fabric, cut a 9"-diameter circle. Fold ¼" of fabric edge to inside all around. With matching thread and sewing needle, sew around outside edge of each circle with a running stitch. Pull thread slightly to form a pouch.

2. Stuff pouch firmly with fiberfill. Pull thread tightly to close circle, adjusting gathers to form a uniformly round ball. Knot thread securely and cut.

3. Poke a tunnel into fiberfill inside ball at gathers. Fill tunnel with hot glue and insert neck into tunnel, pushing down until head almost touches body.

4. Matching bases with corresponding body colors, run a bead of hot glue around top edge of base. Center and place bottom of angel body on glued edge, pressing firmly in place.

5. Cut lace into three equal lengths. With white thread and sewing needle, gather each length along straight edge until edge is approximately 1", or is short enough to wrap around neck with no excess. Knot thread securely. Glue gathered lace around neck to form collar, placing seam at back.

6. Cut ⅛" ribbon into three equal lengths. Tie each length into a small bow; trim ends. Glue one bow to center front of each collar directly under chin. Matching arms with base color, glue arms to sides of body, making shoulders even with edge of collar.

7. Glue one bell to each hand of red angel. Glue tambourine to one hand of navy angel. Glue carols book to both hands of green angel.

8. Poke wires of wings through fabric at center back of each angel body just below collar. Glue wings in place.

—Designs by Vicki Blizzard

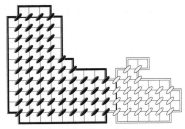

Chubby Angel Arm
16 holes x 11 holes
Cut 12
Stitch 4, reverse 2, as graphed
Stitch 4, reverse 2, replacing
Christmas red with ultra dark pistachio green
Stitch 4, reverse 2, replacing
Christmas red with navy blue

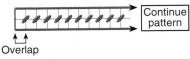

Tambourine
35 holes x 2 holes
Cut 1

Overlap

Continue pattern

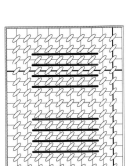

Carols Book Page
11 holes x 14 holes
Cut 2

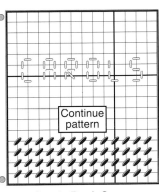

Continue pattern

Carols Book Cover
14 holes x 16 holes
Cut 2

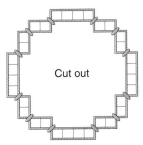

Cut out

Chubby Angel Halo
12 holes x 12 holes
Cut 3

Overlap

Continue pattern

Chubby Angel Base
76 holes x 2 holes
Cut 3
Stitch 1 as graphed,
1 with ultra dark pistachio green,
1 with navy blue

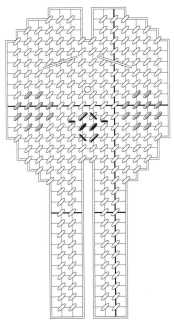

Chubby Angel Head Front & Back
15 holes x 29 holes
Cut 6

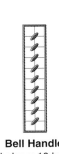

Bell Handle
2 holes x 10 holes
Cut 4

COLOR KEY

#3 Pearl Cotton	Yards
☐ Snow white	9
▨ Dark mahogany #300	2
■ Christmas red #321	14
Navy blue #339	6
▨ Light peach flesh #353	1
Ultra dark pistachio green #890	6
☐ Very light peach flesh #948	12
⁄ Snow white Straight Stitch	
⁄ Christmas red #321 Backstitch	
○ Very light peach flesh #948 French Knot	
6-Strand Embroidery Floss	
⁄ Black #310 Straight Stitch	½
Medium (#16) Braid	
▨ Gold #002	3
Fine (#8) Braid	
⁄ Gold #002 Backstitch	1

Color numbers given are for DMC #3 pearl cotton and 6-strand embroidery floss and Kreinik Medium (#16) Braid and Fine (#8) Braid.

Whimsical Wire-Limb Pins

Here's a great stocking stuffer idea sure to be loved by everyone on this year's gift list!
Santa, Mr. Snowman, Li'l Elf and Mr. Nutcracker are fun to stitch, wear and share!

Skill Level: Intermediate

Materials
Each Pin

- Small amount 10-count plastic canvas
- DMC #3 pearl cotton as listed in color key
- DMC 6-strand embroidery floss as listed in color key
- #22 tapestry needle
- Beading needle
- 3 (8mm) gold jump rings
- 1" gold pin back
- Jewelry pliers
- Hot-glue gun

L'il Elf

- Small amount DMC 6-strand embroidery floss: black #310
- 3 (¼") gold jingle bells
- Seed beads from Mill Hill Products by Gay Bowles Sales, Inc.:
  2 black #02014
  2 gold #02011
- 6" ⅛"-wide green satin ribbon

Mr. Nutcracker

- Kreinik Fine (#8) Braid as listed in color key
- 4mm round ruby cabochon from The Beadery
- Seed beads from Mill Hill Products by Gay Bowles Sales, Inc.:

2 black #02014

2 gold #02011

- 12 small bugle beads from Mill Hill Products by Gay Bowles Sales, Inc.: gold #72011

Mr. Snowman

- Kreinik Medium (#16) Braid as listed in color key

- 10mm x 10mm ruby heart cabochon from The Beadery

- 4mm round ruby cabochon from The Beadery

- 13 seed beads from Mill Hill Products by Gay Bowles Sales, Inc.: black #02014

- 6" ⅛"-wide green satin ribbon

Santa

- Kreinik Fine (#8) Braid as listed in color key

- Small amount DMC 6-strand embroidery floss: bright Christmas red #666

- 4mm ruby round faceted bead from The Beadery

- Seed beads from Mill Hill Products by Gay Bowles Sales, Inc.:

  2 black #02014

  6 gold #02011

- ¼" white pompon

- Small amount white bumpy doll hair

Li'l Elf

1. Cut plastic canvas according to graphs.

2. Stitch pieces following graphs, reversing one shoe before stitching. Overcast head with very light peach flesh and all remaining pieces with adjacent colors.

3. Using beading needle, attach seed beads where indicated on graph with 1 strand black floss. Work embroidery for mouth with 2 strands bright Christmas red floss. Work embroidery on body and shoes with 1 strand bright Christmas red floss. With very light peach flesh, work four Straight Stitches in the same holes for nose.

4. Open jump rings with pliers and insert through three holes indicated on body graph. Insert bottom rings through holes on shoes where indicated on graph; close rings. Insert top ring through hole indicated on head graph; close ring.

5. Using photo as a guide throughout, glue hat to head at a slight angle. Glue one mitten to back of body and one to front of body. Tie a small bow

with green satin ribbon; trim ends. Glue bow to body just under jump ring at neck. Glue jingle bells to tips of shoes and to tip of hat.

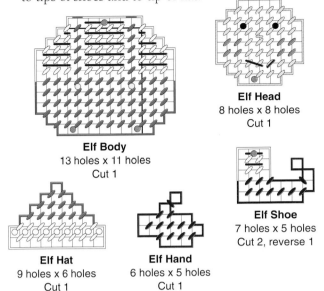

Elf Body
13 holes x 11 holes
Cut 1

Elf Head
8 holes x 8 holes
Cut 1

Elf Shoe
7 holes x 5 holes
Cut 2, reverse 1

Elf Hat
9 holes x 6 holes
Cut 1

Elf Hand
6 holes x 5 holes
Cut 1

COLOR KEY	
LI'L ELF	
#3 Pearl Cotton	**Yards**
■ Bright Christmas red #666	2
▦ Christmas green #699	2
▧ Light carnation #894	¼
□ Very light peach flesh #948	1
□ Bright white #B5200	2
∕ Very light peach flesh #948 Straight Stitch	
○ Bright white #B5200 French Knot	
6-Strand Embroidery Floss	
∕ Bright Christmas red #666 1-strand Straight Stitch	⅙
● Attach jump ring	
● Attach black seed bead	
○ Attach gold seed bead	
Color numbers given are for DMC #3 pearl cotton and 6-strand embroidery floss.	

Mr. Nutcracker

1. Cut plastic canvas according to graphs (page 160).

2. Stitch pieces following graphs, reversing one boot before stitching. Stitch uncoded areas on hat, hat bill, body and boots with black pearl cotton Continental Stitches. Overcast all pieces with adjacent colors.

3. Work embroidery on face with 1 strand floss. Work embroidery on arms, boots and belt with Aztec gold braid. Work embroidery on hat with Christmas green pearl cotton. With very light peach flesh, work four Straight Stitches in the same holes for nose.

4. Using beading needle, attach black seed beads

where indicated on graph with 1 strand black floss. Attach gold seed beads and bugle beads with Aztec gold braid, reversing side of gold seed bead on one arm.

5. Open jump rings with pliers and insert through three holes indicated on body graph. Insert bottom rings through holes on boots where indicated on graph; close rings. Insert top ring through hole indicated on head graph; close ring.

6. Using photo as a guide throughout, glue bill to front of hat, then glue hat to head. Glue one arm to each side of body. Glue cabochon to hat.

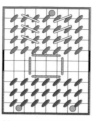

Nutcracker Body
8 holes x 10 holes
Cut 1

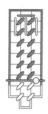

Nutcracker Arm
3 holes x 9 holes
Cut 2, reverse placement
of gold seed bead on 1

Nutcracker Hat Bill
6 holes x 2 holes
Cut 1

Nutcracker Boot
5 holes x 8 holes
Cut 2, reverse 1

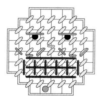

Nutcracker Head
8 holes x 8 holes
Cut 1

Nutcracker Hat
8 holes x 6 holes
Cut 1

COLOR KEY
MR. NUTCRACKER

#3 Pearl Cotton	Yards
■ Christmas green #699	2
■ Very dark royal blue #820	1
□ Very light peach flesh #948	1
□ Bright white #B5200	1
Uncoded areas are black #310 Continental Stitches	2
✐ Black #310 Overcasting	
✐ Christmas green #699 Backstitch	
✐ Very light peach flesh #948 Straight Stitch	

6-Strand Embroidery Floss
✐ Black #310 1-strand Backstitch and Straight Stitch	
✐ Bright Christmas red #666 1-strand Straight Stitch	⅙

Fine (#8) Braid
✐ Aztec gold #202HL Backstitch and Straight Stitch	2
◐ Attach jump ring	
● Attach ruby cabochon	
● Attach black seed bead	
○ Attach gold seed bead	
⬚ Attach gold bugle bead	

Color numbers given are for DMC #3 pearl cotton and 6-strand embroidery floss and Kreinik Fine (#8) Braid.

Mr. Snowman

1. Cut plastic canvas according to graphs (page 161).

2. Stitch pieces following graphs, reversing one mitten and one boot before stitching. Overcast all pieces with adjacent colors.

3. Using beading needle, attach seed beads where indicated on graph with 1 strand black floss. Work embroidery for nose with Aztec gold braid. Work embroidery on hat with Christmas green pearl cotton.

4. Open jump rings with pliers and insert through three holes indicated on body graph. Insert bottom rings through holes on boots where indicated on graph; close rings. Insert top ring through hole indicated on head graph; close ring.

5. Using photo as a guide throughout, glue hat to head at a slight angle. Glue mittens to back of body. Tie a small bow with green satin ribbon; trim ends. Glue bow to center top of body. Glue heart to left side of body.

Snowman Boot
5 holes x 5 holes
Cut 2, reverse 1

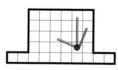

Snowman Hat
10 holes x 5 holes
Cut 1

Snowman Mitten
6 holes x 5 holes
Cut 2, reverse 1

COLOR KEY
MR. SNOWMAN

#3 Pearl Cotton	Yards
■ Christmas green #699	1
■ Very dark royal blue #820	1
Uncoded area on hat is black #310 Continental Stitches	1
Uncoded areas on body and head are bright white #B5200 Continental Stitches	4
✐ Black #310 Overcasting	
✐ Christmas green #699 Backstitch	
✐ Bright white #B5200 Overcasting	

Medium (#16) Braid
✐ Aztec gold #202HL Backstitch	½
◐ Attach jump ring	
● Attach ruby cabochon	
● Attach black seed bead	

Color numbers given are for DMC #3 pearl cotton and Kreinik Medium (#16) Braid.

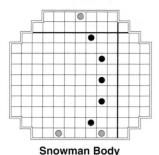

Snowman Body
13 holes x 12 holes
Cut 1

Snowman Head
8 holes x 8 holes
Cut 1

Santa

1. Cut plastic canvas according to graphs5.

2. Stitch pieces following graphs, reversing one boot and one mitten before stitching. Overcast head with very light peach flesh and all remaining pieces with adjacent colors.

3. Work embroidery on face with bright white pearl cotton; work embroidery on boots and body with Aztec gold braid.

4. Using beading needle and following graphs, attach back seed beads with 1 strand black floss, ruby bead with 1 strand bright Christmas red floss and gold seed bead with Aztec gold braid.

5. Open jump rings with pliers and insert through three holes indicated on body graph. Insert bottom rings through holes on boots where indicated on graph; close rings. Insert top ring through hole indicated on head graph; close ring.

6. Wrap a piece of bumpy doll hair four times around two fingers of one hand. Slide loops off fingers and tie in center with a separate 4" length of doll hair. Repeat six to seven times, then glue centers of bundles around bottom of face to form beard. Cut open loops and trim evenly.

7. Using photo as a guide throughout, glue pompon to bottom point of hat tip. Glue top edges of hat tip and hat together. Glue hat to head. Glue one mitten to each side of body.

—*Designs by Vicki Blizzard*

COLOR KEY
SANTA

#3 Pearl Cotton	Yards
■ Bright Christmas red #666	3
■ Christmas green #699	1
▨ Light carnation #894	¼
☐ Very light peach flesh #948	1
☐ Bright white #B5200	2
Uncoded areas are black #310	
Continental Stitches	2
✔ Black #310 Overcasting	
⁄ Bright white #B5200 Straight Stitch	
○ Bright white #B5200 French Knot	
Fine (#8) Braid	
⁄ Aztec gold #202HL Backstitch and	
Straight Stitch	½
● Attach jump ring	
● Attach ruby bead	
● Attach black seed bead	
○ Attach gold seed bead	

Color numbers given are for DMC #3 pearl cotton and Kreinik Fine (#8) Braid.

Santa Hat Tip
4 holes x 5 holes
Cut 1

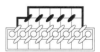

Santa Hat
8 holes x 4 holes
Cut 1

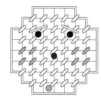

Santa Head
8 holes x 8 holes
Cut 1

Santa Boot
5 holes x 6 holes
Cut 2, reverse 1

Santa Mitten
6 holes x 5 holes
Cut 2, reverse 1

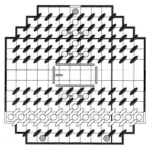

Santa Body
13 holes x 13 holes
Cut 1

Happy Hanukkah

Make this special holiday memorable for your loved ones by including hand-stitched gifts for young and old alike!

"To Life!" Pin

Skill Level: Beginner

Materials

- Small amount 14-count plastic canvas
- DMC 6-strand embroidery floss as listed in color key
- Kreinik Fine (#8) Braid as listed in color key
- #26 tapestry needle
- 20 glass seed beads from Mill Hill Products by Gay Bowles Sales, Inc.: white #00479
- 8 antique glass beads from Mill Hill Products by Gay Bowles Sales, Inc.: blue #03047
- 1" pin back
- Hot-glue gun

Instructions

1. Cut plastic canvas according to graphs (page 165).

2. Stitch pieces following graphs, Continental Stitching uncoded areas with 4 stands white floss. Embroider Star of David when background stitching is completed. Overcast pieces with silver braid, using two to three stitches per hole to cover canvas.

3. Attach a 12" length of 1 strand white floss with a

Lark's Head Knot (Fig. 1) where indicated on star. Thread 14 beads on each end of floss as follows: two white, one blue, two white, one blue, etc., ending with two white. Thread floss ends from front to back at holes indicated on Chai symbol graph with red dots. Fasten ends securely on backside.

4. Glue pin back to backside of Star of David.

—Design by Vicki Blizzard

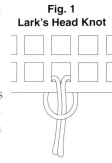

**Fig. 1
Lark's Head Knot**

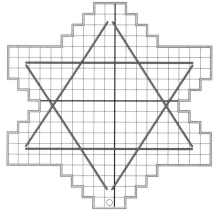

Star of David
19 holes x 19 holes
Cut 1

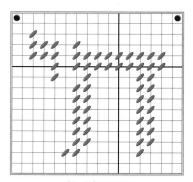

Chai Symbol
16 holes x 15 holes
Cut 1

COLOR KEY	
"TO LIFE!" PIN	
6-Strand Embroidery Floss	**Yards**
Uncoded areas are white Continental Stitches	4
○ White 1-strand Lark's Head Knot	
Fine (#8) Braid	
■ Blue #006	2
╱ Silver #001 Overcasting	2
╱ Blue #006 Backstitch	
Color numbers given are for Kreinik Fine (#8) Braid.	

Star of David Coaster Set

Skill Level: Beginner

Materials

- ¼ sheet 7-count plastic canvas
- 5 Uniek 7-count plastic canvas hexagons
- Uniek Needloft plastic canvas yarn as listed in color key
- #16 tapestry needle

Instructions

1. Cut holder front and back from one hexagon, cutting through middle of center bar to so hexagon can be used for both pieces; cut holder sides and bottom from plastic canvas and coasters from four remaining hexagons according to graphs (pages 164 and 165). Holder bottom will remain unstitched.

2. Stitch pieces following graphs. Work royal Backstitches over completed background stitching. Overcast coasters with royal, working two stitches in each hole to cover points.

3. With royal, Whipstitch holder sides to unstitched bottom, then Whipstitch front and back to sides and bottom, working two stitches in each hole and easing to fit. Overcast top edges of holder with white.

—Design by Vicki Blizzard

COLOR KEY	
STAR OF DAVID COASTER SET	
Plastic Canvas Yarn	**Yards**
☐ White #41	32
▨ Bright blue #60	6
✎ Royal #32 Backstitch and Overcasting and Whipstitching	17
Color numbers given are for Uniek Needloft plastic canvas yarn.	

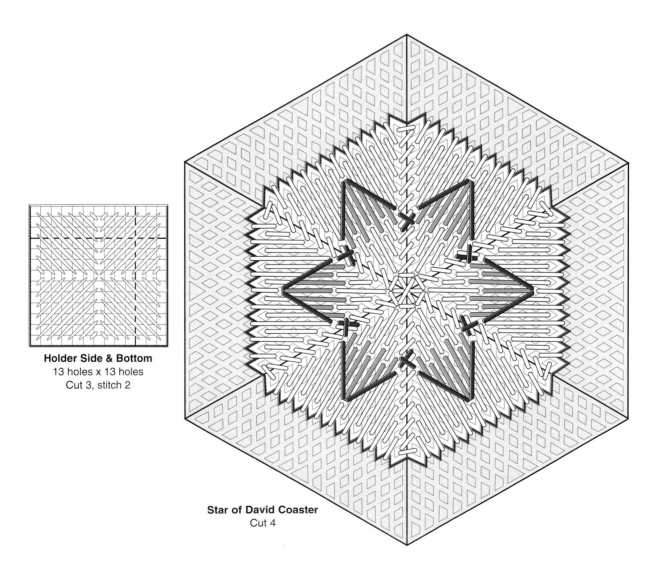

Holder Side & Bottom
13 holes x 13 holes
Cut 3, stitch 2

Star of David Coaster
Cut 4

Shalom Door Sign & Mezuzah Case

Skill Level: Beginner

Materials

- 3 sheets Uniek Quick-Count 7-count plastic canvas
- Red Heart Super Saver worsted weight yarn Art. E301 as listed in color key
- ¹⁄₁₆"-wide Rainbow Gallery Plastic Canvas 10 Metallic Needlepoint Yarn as listed in color key
- #16 tapestry needle
- 3 (10mm) silver jump rings
- Needle-nose jewelry pliers
- Seam sealant
- Sawtooth hanger
- Hot-glue gun

Instructions

1. Cut plastic canvas according to graphs (pages 165–167), cutting out center area on sign front only. Sign back will remain unstitched.

2. Stitch insert following graph, working Cross Stitches first, then filling in uncoded area with white Continental Stitches. Work silver Backstitches when background stitching is completed. Do not Overcast.

3. Work sign front and case pieces following graphs. With royal, Overcast inside edges of front, then work silver Backstitches.

4. Center insert behind opening on front; glue in place. Whipstitch front to unstitched back with royal. Attach jump ring where indicated on graph. Center and glue sawtooth hanger under top edge of sign.

5. Using royal throughout, Overcast bottom edges of lid sides and top edges of case sides. Whipstitch lid sides together then lid sides to lid top. Whipstitch case sides together, then case sides to case bottom.

6. Attach one jump ring to lower corner of case sides and remaining jump ring to upper corner of lid sides where indicated on graphs. Cut an 8"

Holder Front & Back
Cut in half before stitching

↑
Cut here

length of silver yarn. Tie one end to case jump ring.
Thread remaining end through jump ring on sign,
then tie to lid jump ring. Knot ends securely, then
trim close to knots. Apply seam sealant.

7. Insert scroll in case, then place lid on case.

—Designs by Vicki Blizzard

Case Lid Side
9 holes x 7 holes
Cut 4

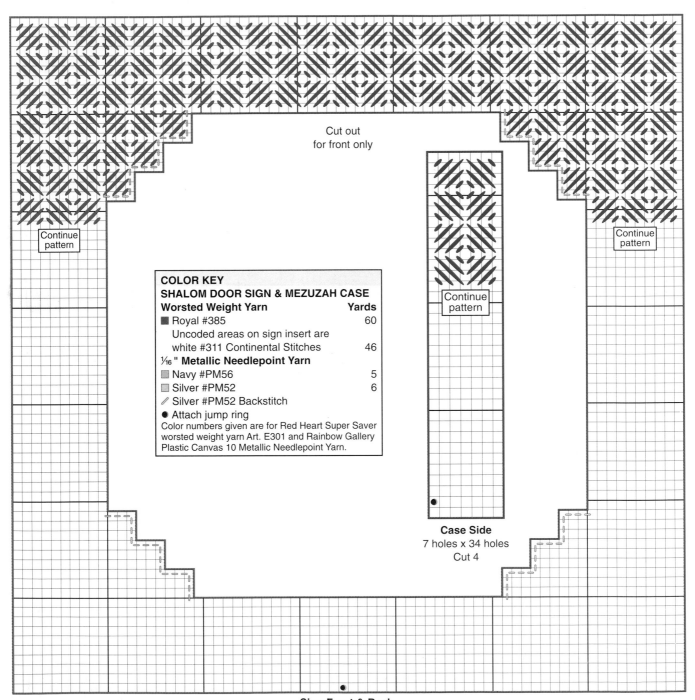

Cut out
for front only

Continue
pattern

Continue
pattern

Continue
pattern

COLOR KEY
SHALOM DOOR SIGN & MEZUZAH CASE

Worsted Weight Yarn	Yards
■ Royal #385	60
Uncoded areas on sign insert are white #311 Continental Stitches	46

1/16" Metallic Needlepoint Yarn

▨ Navy #PM56	5
▨ Silver #PM52	6
⁄ Silver #PM52 Backstitch	
● Attach jump ring	

Color numbers given are for Red Heart Super Saver
worsted weight yarn Art. E301 and Rainbow Gallery
Plastic Canvas 10 Metallic Needlepoint Yarn.

Case Side
7 holes x 34 holes
Cut 4

Sign Front & Back
70 holes x 70 holes
Cut 2, stitch 1

Case Bottom
7 holes x 7 holes
Cut 1

Case Lid Top
9 holes x 9 holes
Cut 1

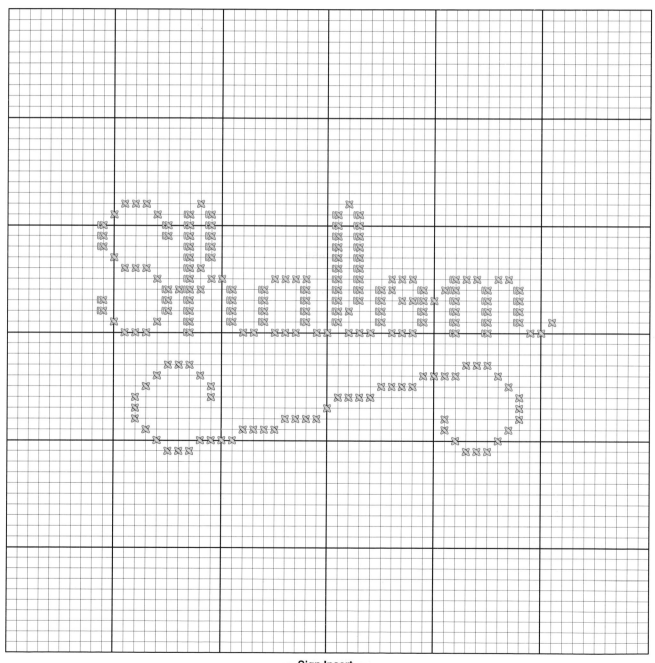

Sign Insert
60 holes x 60 holes
Cut 1

Mini Holiday Quilts

...ocks have never been more popular! This engaging set of six holiday quilt blocks, ...ed with decorative buttons, can be used as pins or refrigerator magnets.

Skill Level: Beginner

Materials

- Small amount 14-count plastic canvas
- DMC 6-strand embroidery floss as listed in color key
- #24 tapestry needle
- 6 ceramic buttons by Mill Hill Products from Gay Bowles Sales, Inc.:

  Bunny #86043

  Watermelon heart #86078

  Pumpkin heart #86083

  Flag heart #86125

  Santa heart #86161

  Red leaf #86189

- Magnets or pin backs as desired
- Hot-glue gun

Instructions

1. Cut plastic canvas according to graphs (pages 169 and 170).

2. Following graphs, cut floss in 1 yard lengths and stitch with entire 6-strand length, weaving ends in farther than usual to keep ends from slipping out. Overcast pieces following graphs.

3. With matching floss, sew buttons to center of each block as follows: bunny on Flying Geese, watermelon heart on Many-Pointed Star, pumpkin heart on Hole in a Barn Door, flag heart on Ohio Star, Santa heart on Arrow Point and red leaf on Indian Plumes.

4. Glue a magnet or pin back to wrong side of each mini quilt.

—Designs by Joan Green

COLOR KEY
FLYING GEESE

6-Strand Embroidery Floss	Yards
▨ Medium shell pink #223	3
☐ Cream #712	3
▨ Dark antique blue #930	2

Color numbers given are for DMC 6-strand embroidery floss.

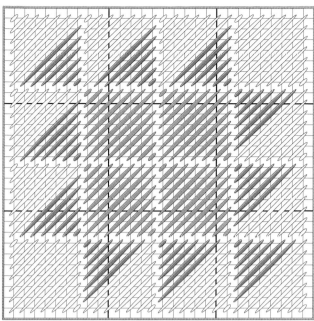

Flying Geese
29 holes x 29 holes
Cut 1

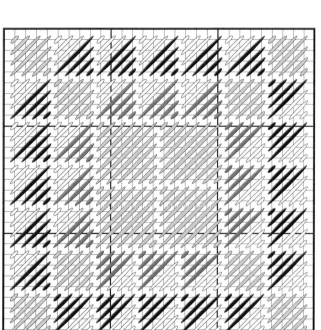

Indian Plumes
29 holes x 29 holes
Cut 1

COLOR KEY
INDIAN PLUMES

6-Strand Embroidery Floss	Yards
▨ Coral #350	1
☐ Cream #712	2
▨ Christmas gold #783	3
■ Garnet #815	3

Color numbers given are for DMC 6-strand embroidery floss.

COLOR KEY
MANY-POINTED STAR

6-Strand Embroidery Floss	Yards
■ Dark carnation #601	3
☐ Cream #712	3
▨ Dark willow green #986	2

Color numbers given are for DMC 6-strand embroidery floss.

Many-Pointed Star
29 holes x 29 holes
Cut 1

COLOR KEY
OHIO STAR

6-Strand Embroidery Floss	Yards
■ Christmas red #321	3
☐ Cream #712	3
■ Very dark navy blue #823	2

Color numbers given are for DMC 6-strand embroidery floss.

Ohio Star
29 holes x 29 holes
Cut 1

Hole in a Barn Door
29 holes x 29 holes
Cut 1

COLOR KEY
HOLE IN A BARN DOOR

6-Strand Embroidery Floss	Yards
■ Black #310	3
☐ Deep canary #444	2
▨ Bright pumpkin #947	3

Color numbers given are for DMC 6-strand embroidery floss.

COLOR KEY
ARROW POINT

6-Strand Embroidery Floss	Yards
■ Christmas red #321	2
▨ Bright Christmas green #700	2
☐ Cream #712	2
■ Ultra dark pistachio green #890	2

Color numbers given are for DMC 6-strand embroidery floss.

Arrow Point
29 holes x 29 holes
Cut 1

Snowman Welcome

Invite one and all into your home with this bright snowman welcome sign! Work him in the colors shown for Christmas, or choose colors to match your decor.

Skill Level: Beginner

Materials

- 1 sheet 7-count plastic canvas
- Uniek Needloft plastic canvas yarn as listed in color key

Instructions

1. Cut plastic canvas according to graphs.

2. Stitch snowman, scarf top, scarf bottom and pockets. Using white, add French Knots to snowman's sweater when background stitching is complete.

3. Using Christmas red, Overcast snowman's sweater. Using white, Overcast snowman's head and bottom of body.

4. Using Christmas green through step 5, Overcast scarf pieces, snowman's hat, and pocket top and bottom edges. Whipstitch pocket edges to sweater where indicated.

5. Tack scarf bottom and scarf top to right side of scarf where indicated. Add three large, loose French knots to cover ends of scarf top and bottom.

6. Using black throughout, stitch Smyrna Stitch onto buttons. Overcast edges; add second layer of Smyrna Stitch to attach buttons to snowman.

—Design by Mary T. Cosgrove

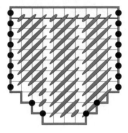

Pocket
10 holes x 11 holes
Cut 2

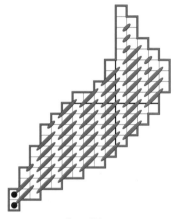

Scarf Top
15 holes x 19 holes
Cut 1

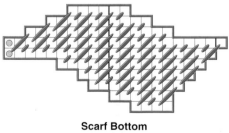

Scarf Bottom
21 holes x 10 holes
Cut 1

COLOR KEY

Plastic Canvas Yarn	Yards
■ Black #00	7
■ Christmas red #02	24
■ Christmas green #28	19
Uncoded areas are white #41 Continental Stitches	26
✎ Christmas red #02 Straight Stitch	
⁄ White #41 Straight Stitch and Overcasting	
● Christmas green #28 French Knot	
○ White #41 French Knot	
● Attach pocket	
● Attach scarf top	
● Attach scarf bottom	
◇ Attach button	
Color numbers given are for Uniek Needloft plastic canvas yarn.	

Snowman
58 holes x 90 holes
Cut 1

Stitch Guide

Use the following diagrams to expand your plastic canvas stitching. For each diagram, bring needle up through canvas at the red number one and go back down through the canvas at the red number two. The second stitch is numbered in green. Always bring needle up through the canvas at odd numbers and take it back down through the canvas at the even numbers.

Background Stitches

The following stitches are used for filling in large areas of canvas. The Continental Stitch is the most commonly used stitch. Other stitches, such as the Condensed Mosaic and Scotch Stitch, fill in large areas of canvas more quickly than the Continental Stitch because their stitches cover a larger area of canvas.

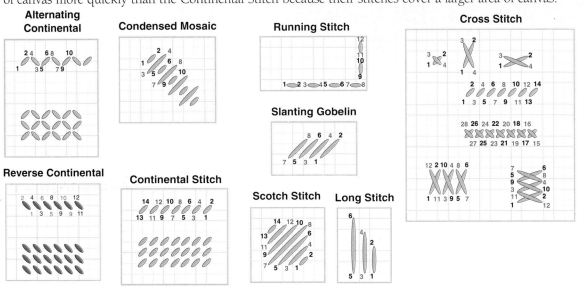

Embroidery Stitches

Embroidery stitches are worked on top of a stitched area to add detail and beauty to your project. Embroidery stitches are usually worked with one strand of yarn, several strands of pearl cotton or several strands of embroidery floss.

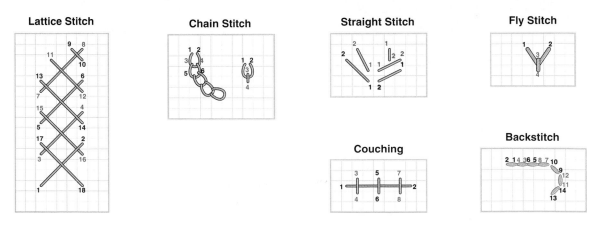

Embroidery Stitches

French Knot

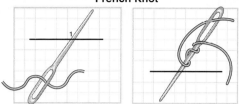

Bring needle up through piece.
Wrap yarn around needle 2 or 3 times,
depending on desired size of knot; take needle
back through piece through same hole.

Lazy Daisy

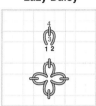

Bring yarn needle up through
canvas, then back down in same
hole, leaving a small loop.

Then, bring needle up inside
loop; take needle back down
through piece on other side of
loop.

Specialty Stitches

The following stitches can be worked either on top of a previously stitched area or directly onto the
canvas. Like the embroidery stitches, these too add wonderful detail and give your stitching additional
interest and texture.

Diamond Eyelet

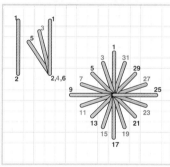

For each stitch, bring needle
up at odd numbers around
outside and take needle down
through canvas at center hole.

Smyrna Cross

Satin Stitch

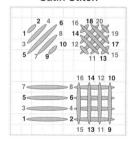

This stitch gives a
"padded" look to
your work.

Finishing Stitches

Both of these stitches are
used to finish the outer edges
of the canvas. Overcasting
is done to finish one edge
at a time. Whipstitch is
used to stitch two pieces of
canvas together. For both
Overcasting and Whip-
stitching, work one stitch in
each hole along straight edges
and inside corners, and two
or three stitches in outside
corners.

Overcast/Whipstitch

Loop Stitch or Turkey Loop Stitch

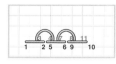

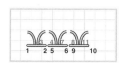

The top diagram shows this stitch left intact.
This is an effective stitch for giving a project
dimensional hair. The bottom diagram
demonstrates the cut loop stitch. Because
each stitch is anchored, cutting it will not
cause the stitches to come out. A group of
cut loop stitches gives a fluffy, soft look and
feel to your project.

Project & Designer Index

Special thanks to each of the following designers whose work and creativity is expressed in the projects featured in this book.

Arickx, Angie 7, 12, 79, 100, 140
Baggett, Vickie 14
Beck, Roseanna 68
Blizzard, Vicki 33, 36, 105, 113,
  127, 135, 138, 143, 144, 155, 158, 162, 163
Bond America 83
Britton, Janna 12, 111
Celia Lange Designs 16, 17, 38, 49
Cosgrove, Mary T. 56, 125, 171
Dobbs, Phyllis 60
Fanton, Darla 42
Fox, E. Wayne 122
Gibney, Conn Baker 70, 74
Green, Joan 10, 65, 168
Kauffman, Judi 40, 84, 87, 117, 125, 137, 145
Kennebeck, Kathleen 120
Krob, Carol 23, 86, 92
Leck, Cherie Marie 25
Loffredo, Kristine 70, 142
Macor, Alida 110
Marshall, Nancy 27, 81, 102, 110, 147
Nartowicz, Carol 95, 97, 100
O'Donnell, Kathleen Marie 8, 18, 47
Ricioli, Terry 107
Scott, Laura 66
Smith, Linda L. 123
Suber, Kimberly 9
Telesca, Marianne 127
Thacker, Ruby 19, 20, 29, 54, 97
Trumball, Pat 84
Tunnell, Elayne 31
Vanetta, Jeanette 58
Wilcox, Michelle 69, 76, 78,
  102, 148, 150, 152
Wirth, Kathy 153
Wyszynski, Linda 52, 89
Yorston, Debi 15